Nature's Art

The artwork and story of my first year as an artist

Nathalie Goss

Nature's Art

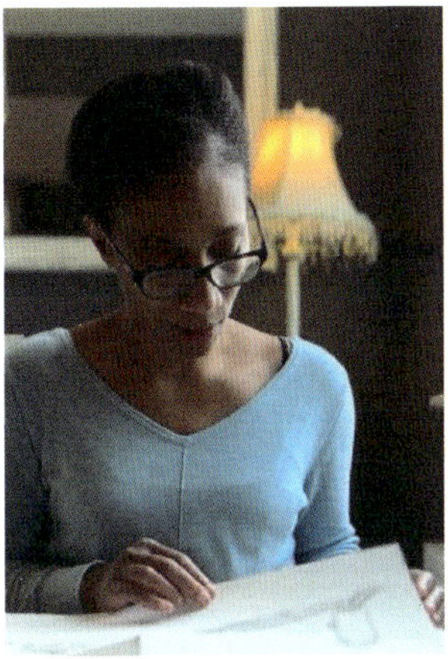

Original artwork, inspired by nature and featuring countryside flora and fauna.

Nathalie Goss is a French artist with a passion for capturing British wildlife.

A stunning collection of Nathalie Goss' hand-drawn, gouache painted pieces, uniquely collaged with photography of local flora.

Nathalie Goss

Dedication

Thank you to my supportive husband and my wonderful daughters

Egg

Where life begins.

Signs of life begin popping up around the garden and when I'm out and about. Spring can kind of, spring up out of nowhere and surprise me sometimes. That walk I take everyday... the one where it's so easy to not stop to take notice of the life popping up around me... then a snowdrop surprises me out of nowhere. Then it's the daffodils turn to tap me on the shoulder.

I originally drew this egg for Easter time. It featured on one of my greetings cards that sold in local gift shops.

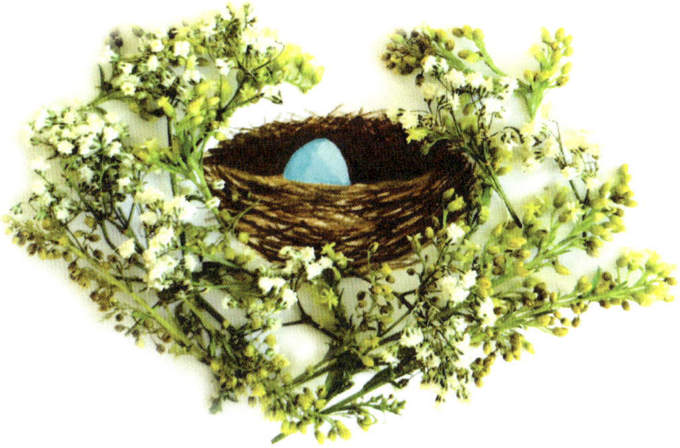

Nest

Painted with gouache. Finished with baby breath and yellow dried flowers.

Butterfly

Sometimes tiny details in nature bring me back to my childhood. Things like the touch of a daisy's delicate white ray floret, when my daughters bring me daisy chains they have carefully been crafting.

The smell of freshly cut grass is just as nostalgic, evoking memories of walking through parks on summer holidays.

Le Papillon Bleu with my daughters' hand picked daisies, marks the beginning of summer.

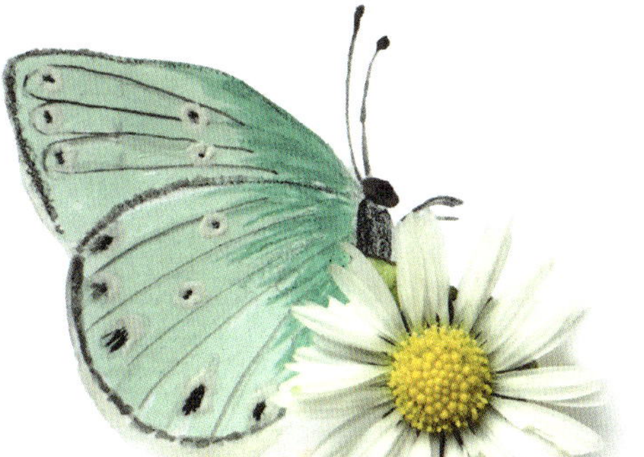

Le Papillon Bleu

Painted with gouache. Finished with hand picked daisies.

Dunnock

The leaves have flown from the trees, but the young nestlings don't seem close to flying the nest.

Mother dunnock seems in no rush. She will keep her little ones warm and safe in the family nest until the time comes.

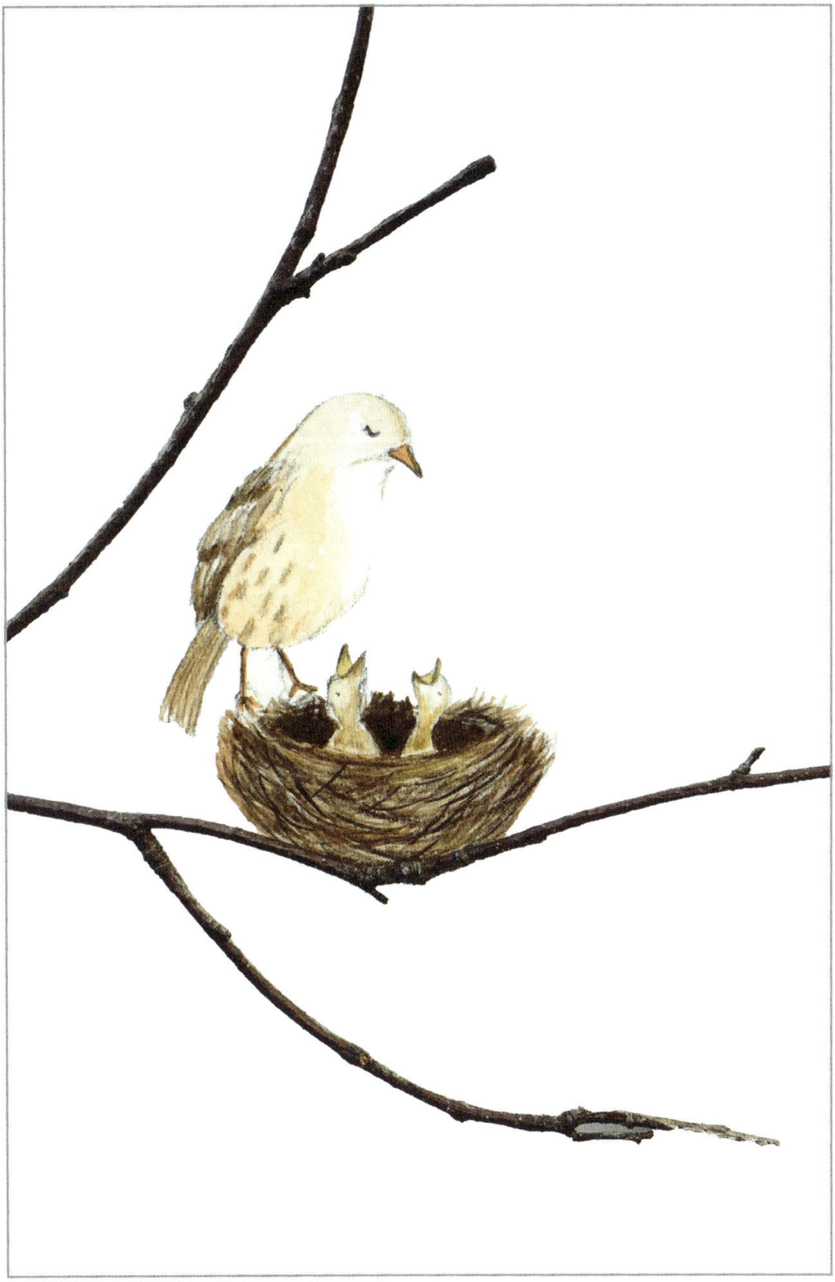

Dunnock Mum and her little ones

Painted in gouache. Sitting on a twig.

Bunnies

Curled up under a carrot leaf, these two bunnies keep each other company.

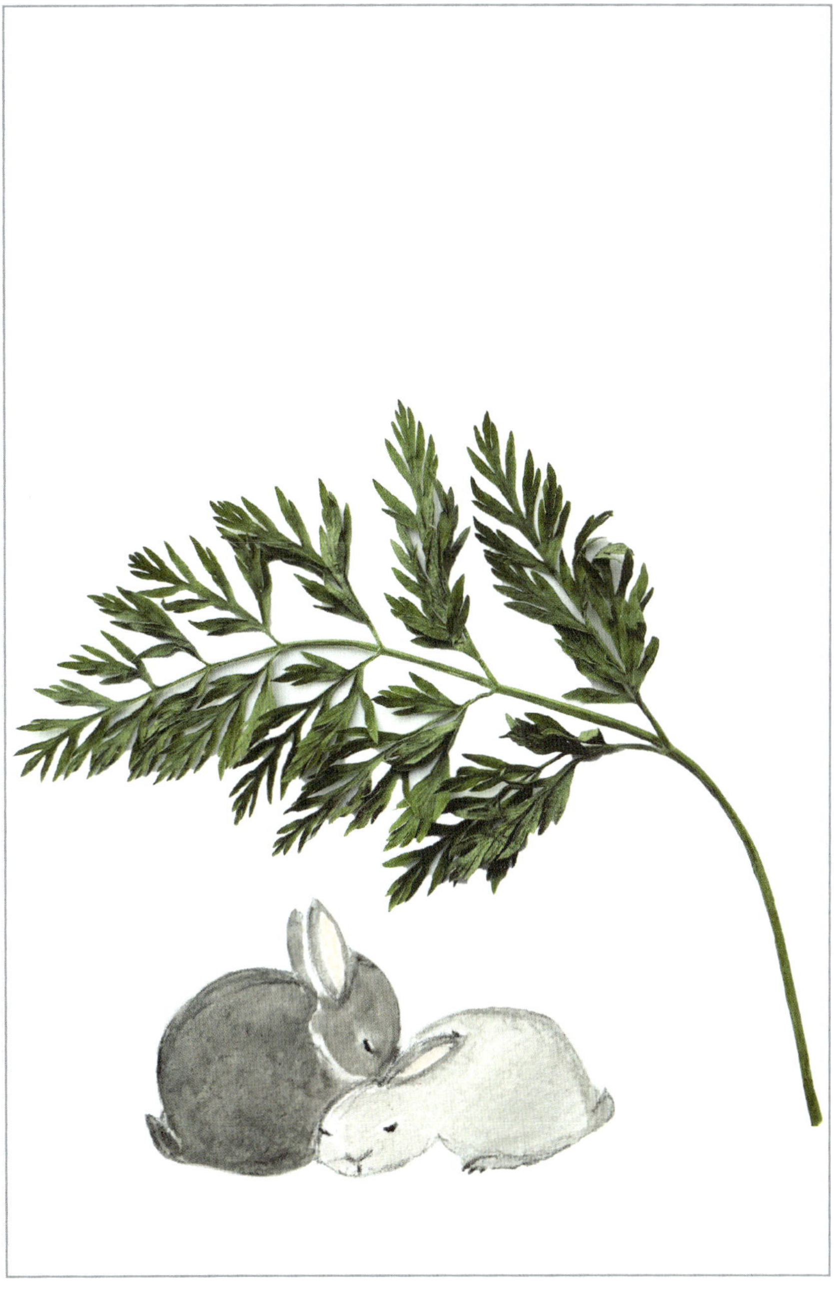

Little Bunnies

Painted with gouache. Finished with carrot leaf.

Puffins

I drew these puffins after receiving a postcard from my mother-in law, who lives in Scotland.

I've never seen puffins in the wild, but I was fascinated by their distinctive, bold markings and beautiful bills. What I love even more is that they mate with the same partner throughout their lifetime.

The parrots of the sea.

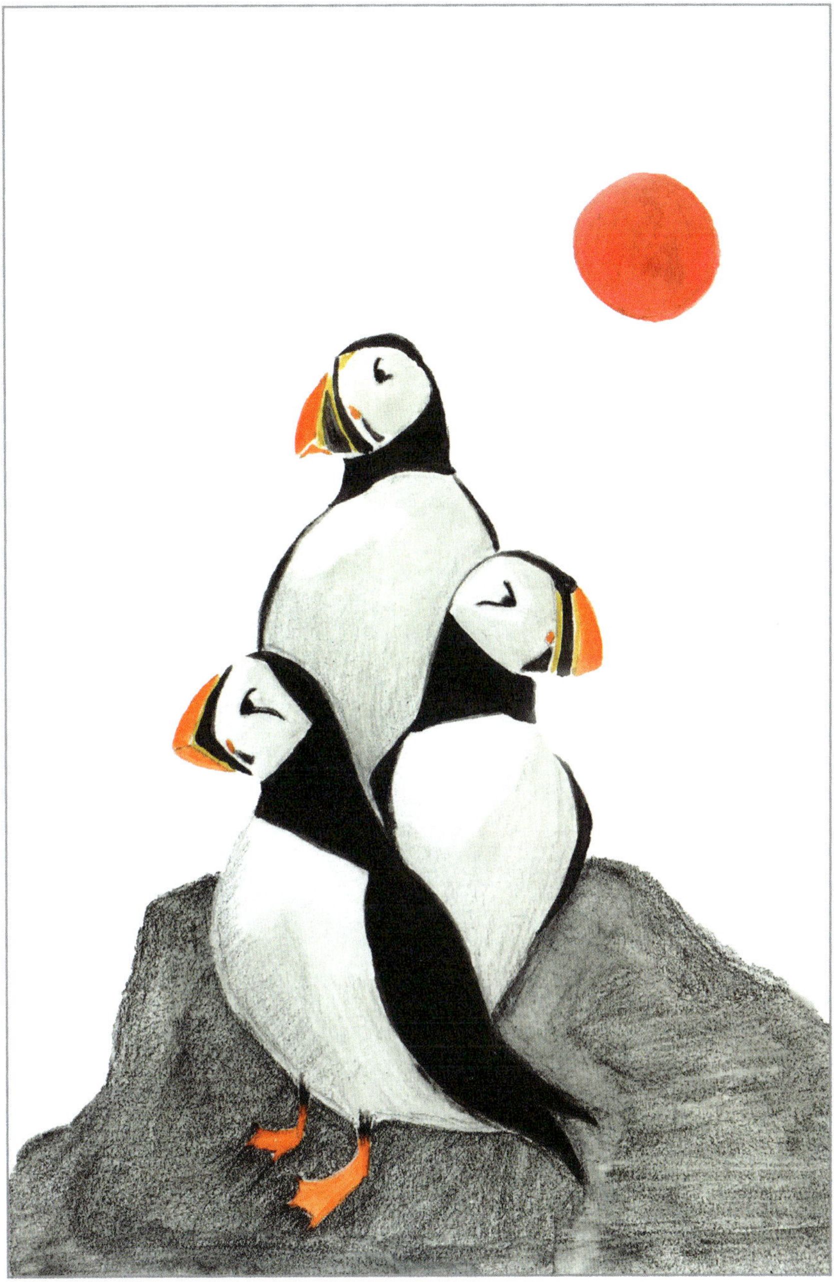

Puffins

Painted with gouache and pencil.

Badger

Time for a nap.

There's always so much to do... a list as long as my arm.

But first on the list...

Nap-time.

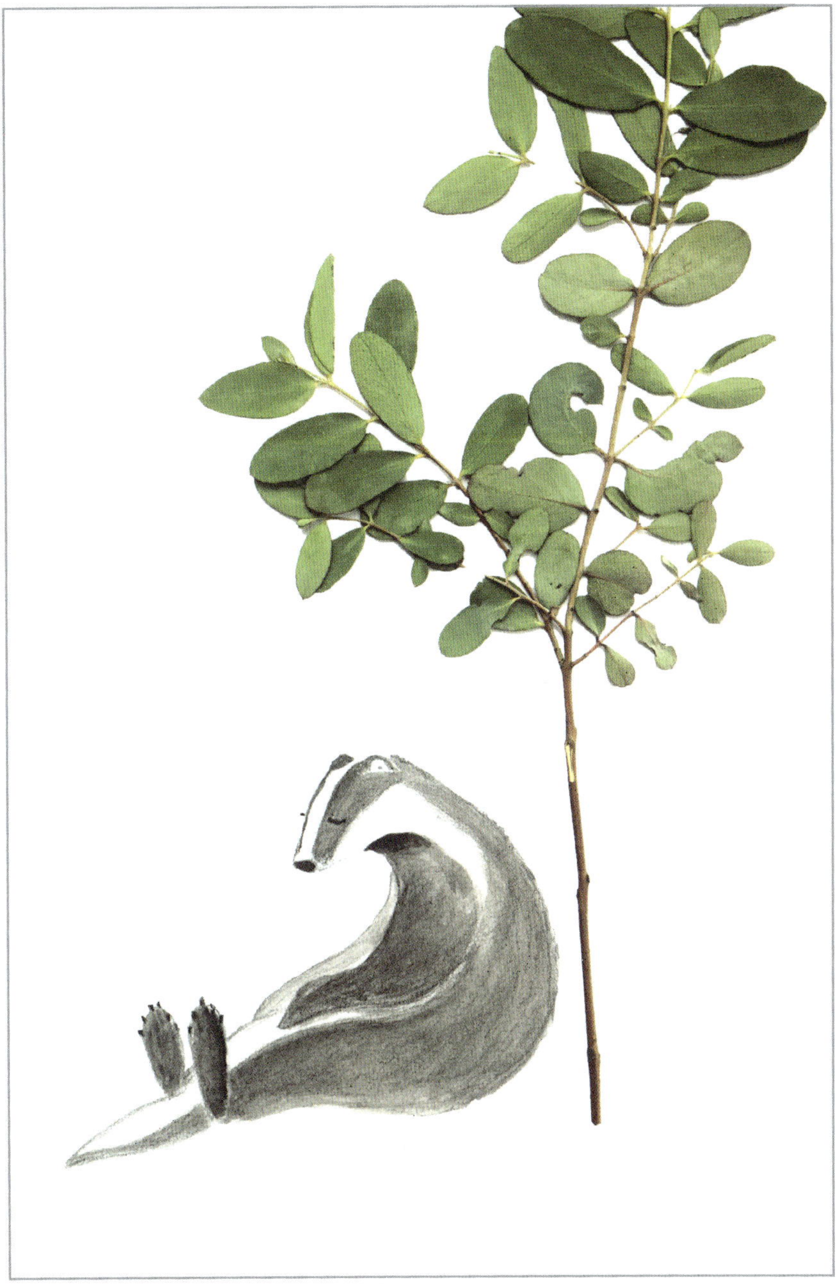

Dozing Badger

Painted in gouache. Finished with eucalyptus.

Rabbits

My youngest daughter absolutely loves spotting the hot air balloons in the summer skies.

She loves rabbits too, so a nest of rabbits rising up felt like the perfect combination for her birthday card.

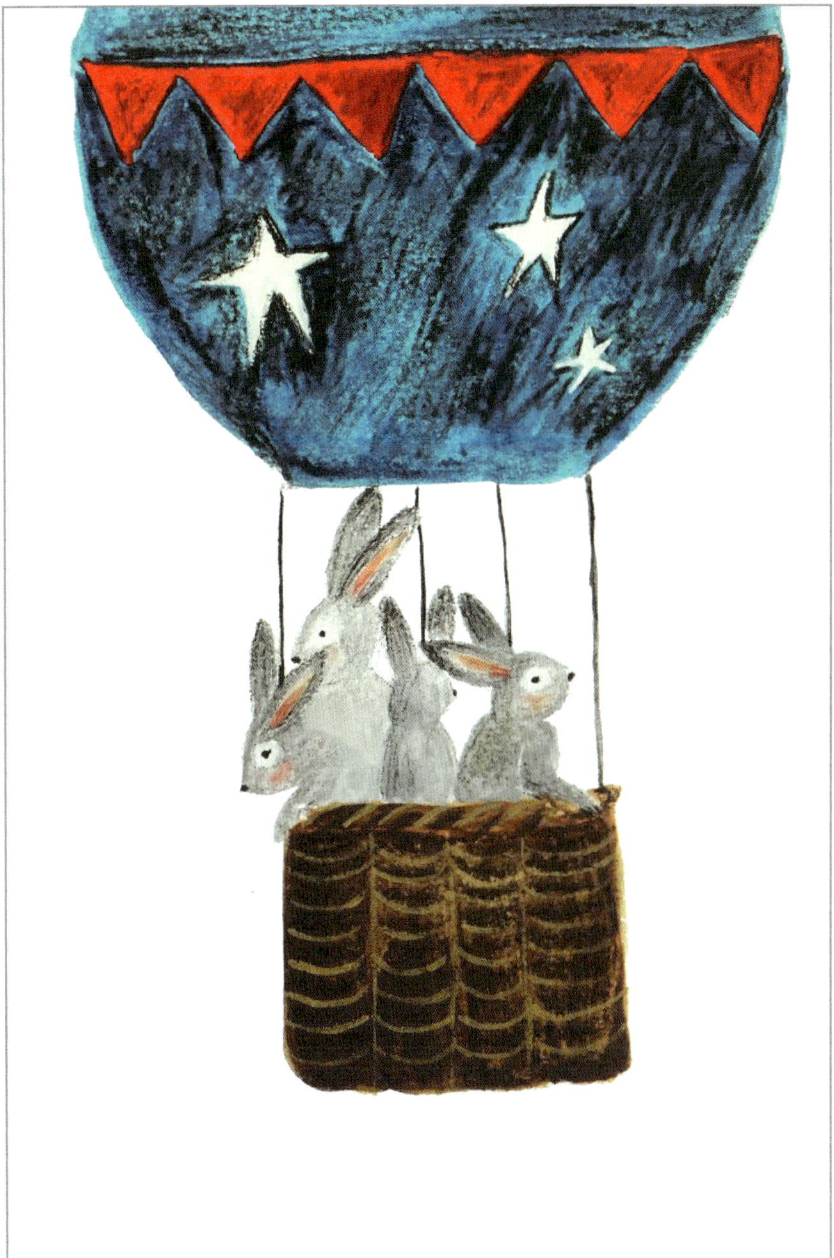

Hot air balloon ride

Painted in gouache.

Seagulls

Seaside, seagull,

Sun and sand.

Fish and chips,

Close at hand.

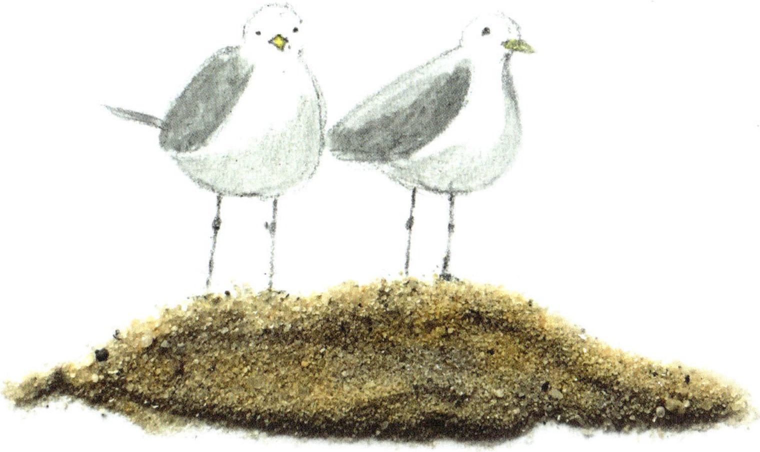

Seagulls

Painted with gouache. Finished with sand.

Fish

This is one of my rare drawings without flora or fauna. Adding sand or seaweed wouldn't have complemented the illustration, so these fish stand alone.

Fish often remind me of my childhood, spending time in the Caribbean at my grandma's house and going fishing with my cousin at the local port.

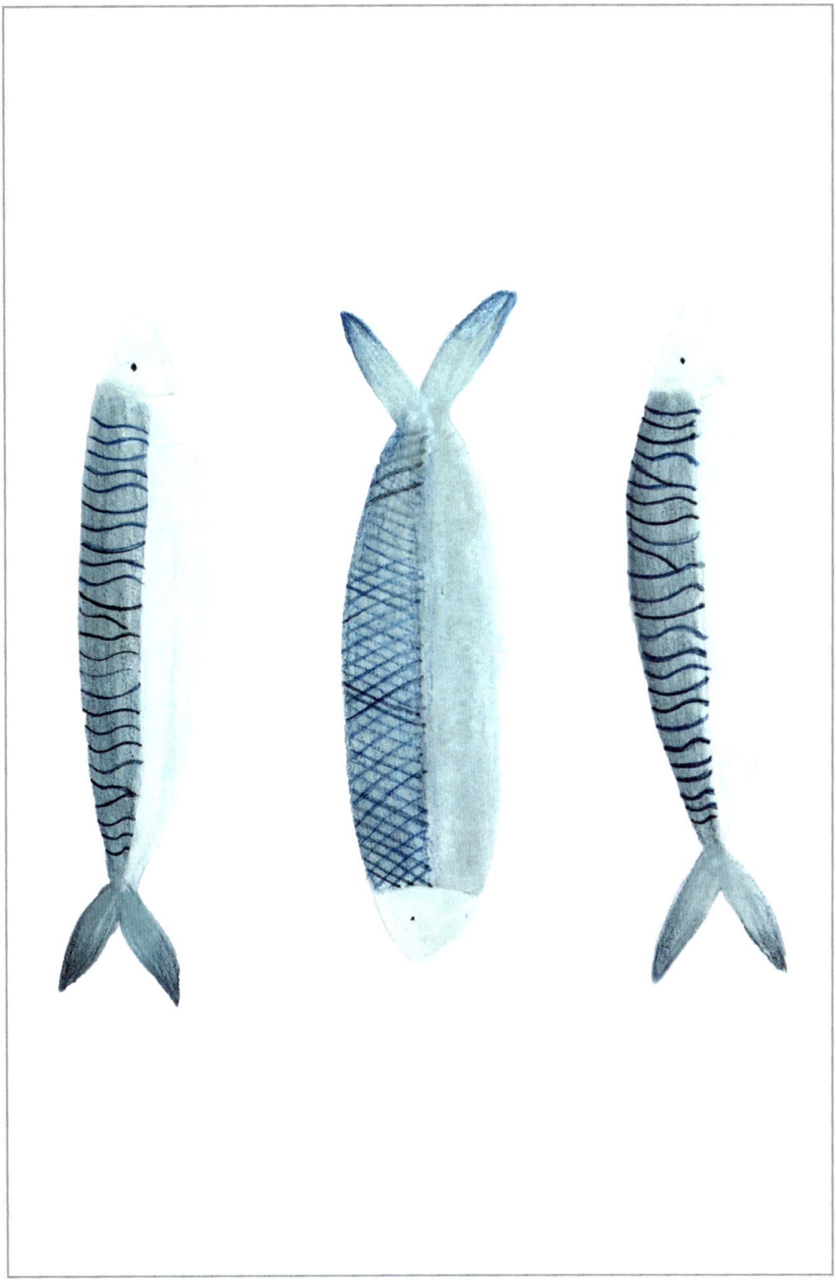

1, 2, 3 Fish

Painted with gouache.

Puffins

Summer is here.

A season where time itself seems to stay still as the long summer days roll into the evenings.

Relax and enjoy the quietness of the sea with someone special.

Puffins by the seaside

Painted with oil pastel.

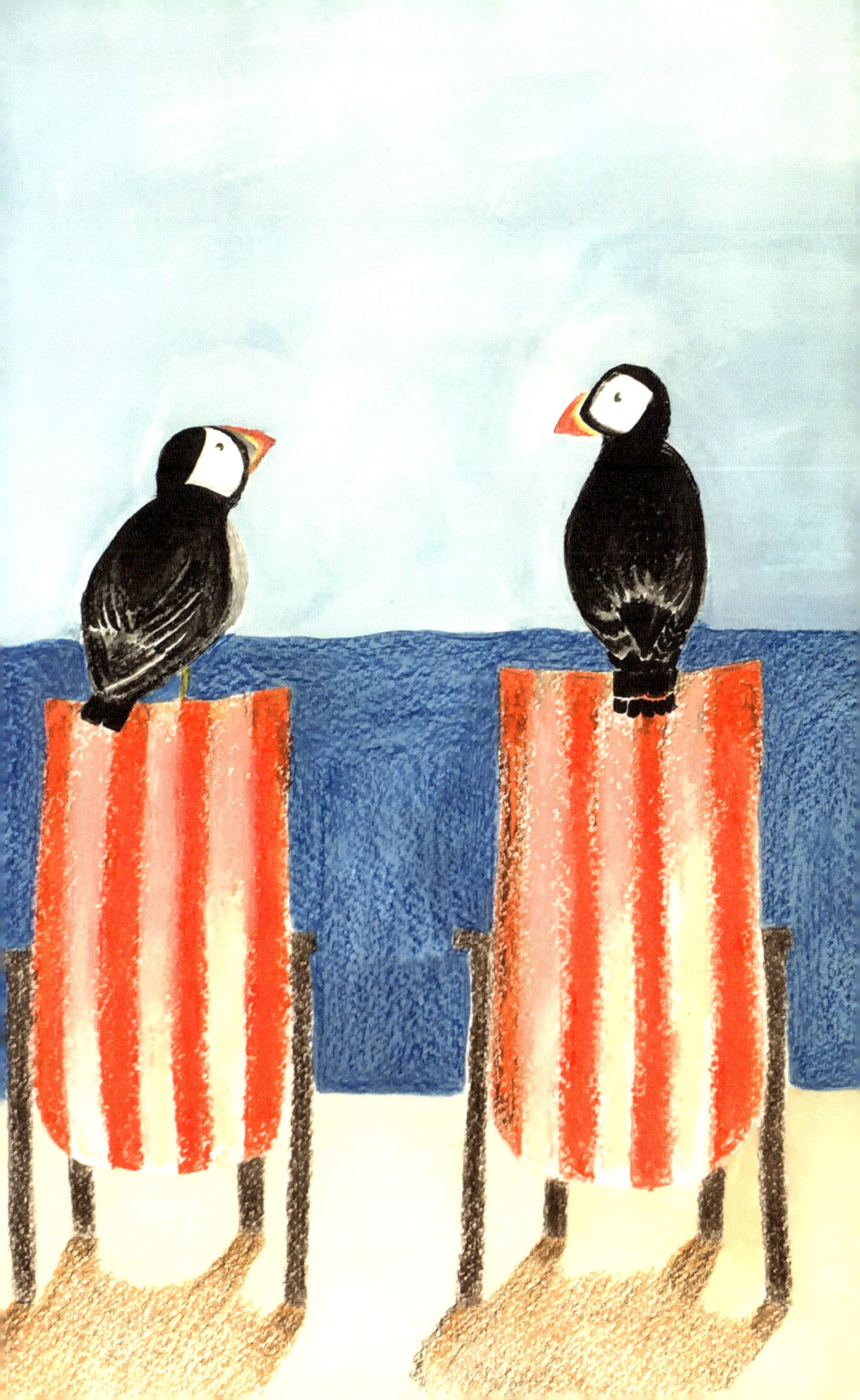

Mouse

Little brown mouse is sheltering from the hot mid-afternoon sun.

Oh hello there.

Tell me, do you like butter?

This buttercup will tell me.

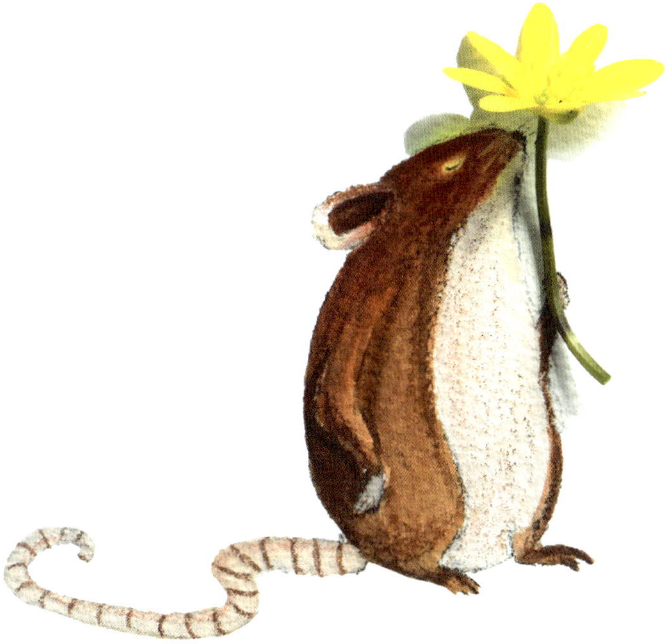

Little Mouse

Painted with gouache. Finished with a handpicked buttercup.

Fox

The days start to shorten and the nights become colder.

A stunning crimson for the autumnal beholder.

Autumnal fox with his reddish fur, sits elegantly facing

the first falling leaves of autumn.

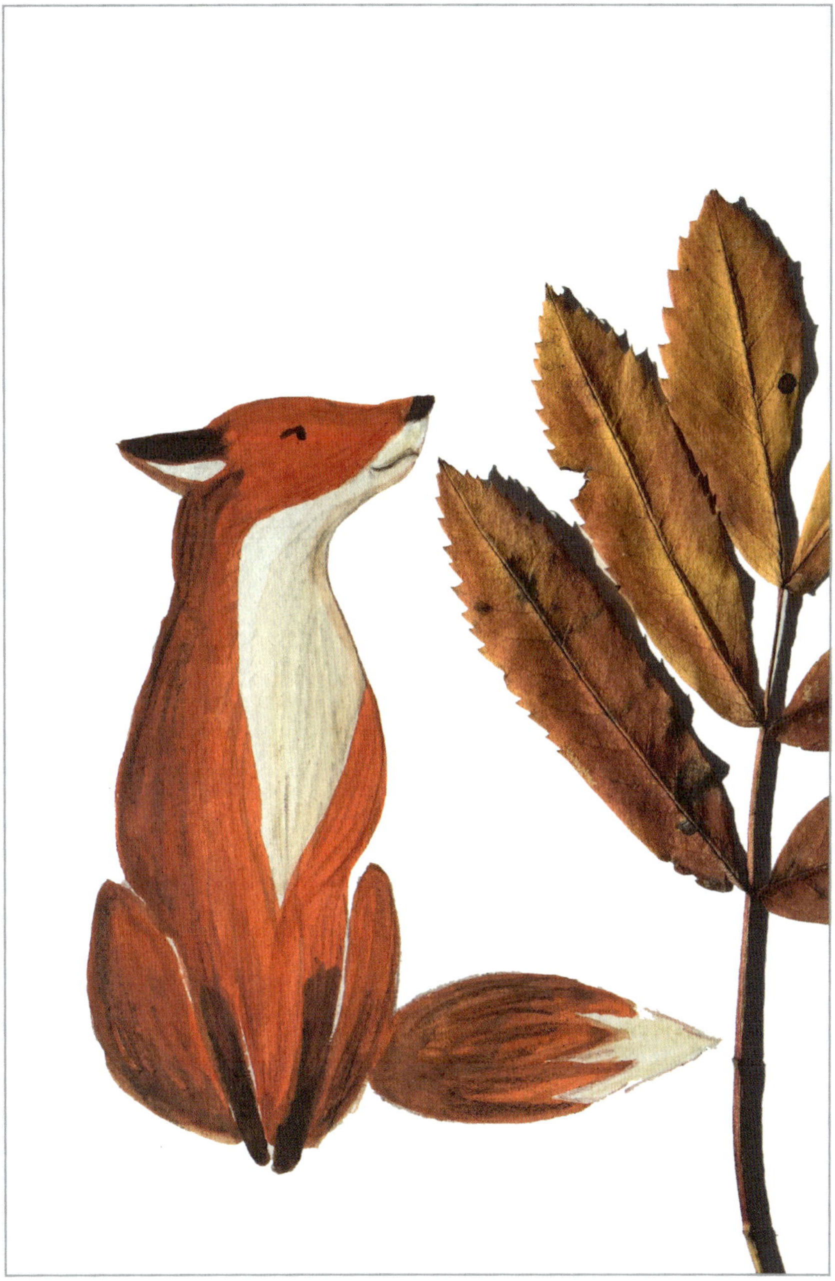

Autumnal Fox

Painted in gouache. Finished with fallen leaves.

Hedgehog

Can you see the tiny brush strokes of her spines?

Sometimes it can take me longer to work on the details of a particular animal coat than the whole drawing itself.

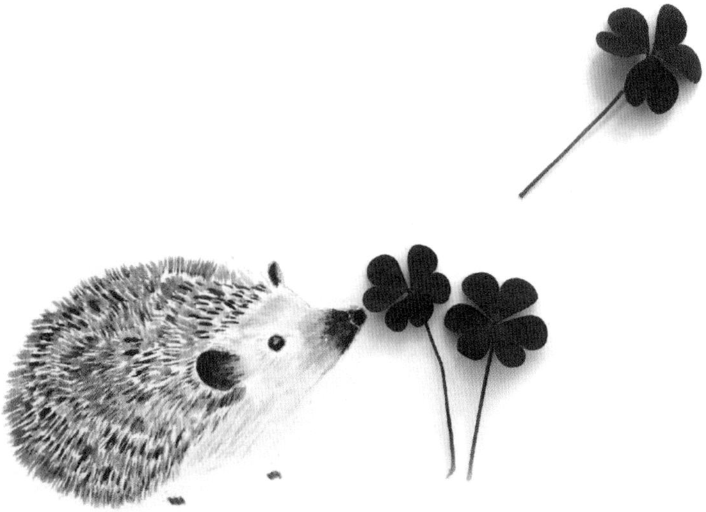

Creeping Hedgehog

Painted with gouache. Finished with creeping woodsorrel.

Starling

I started learning to draw just a couple of years ago.

With this starling, I used a new technique...

everything done with just a 6B pencil.

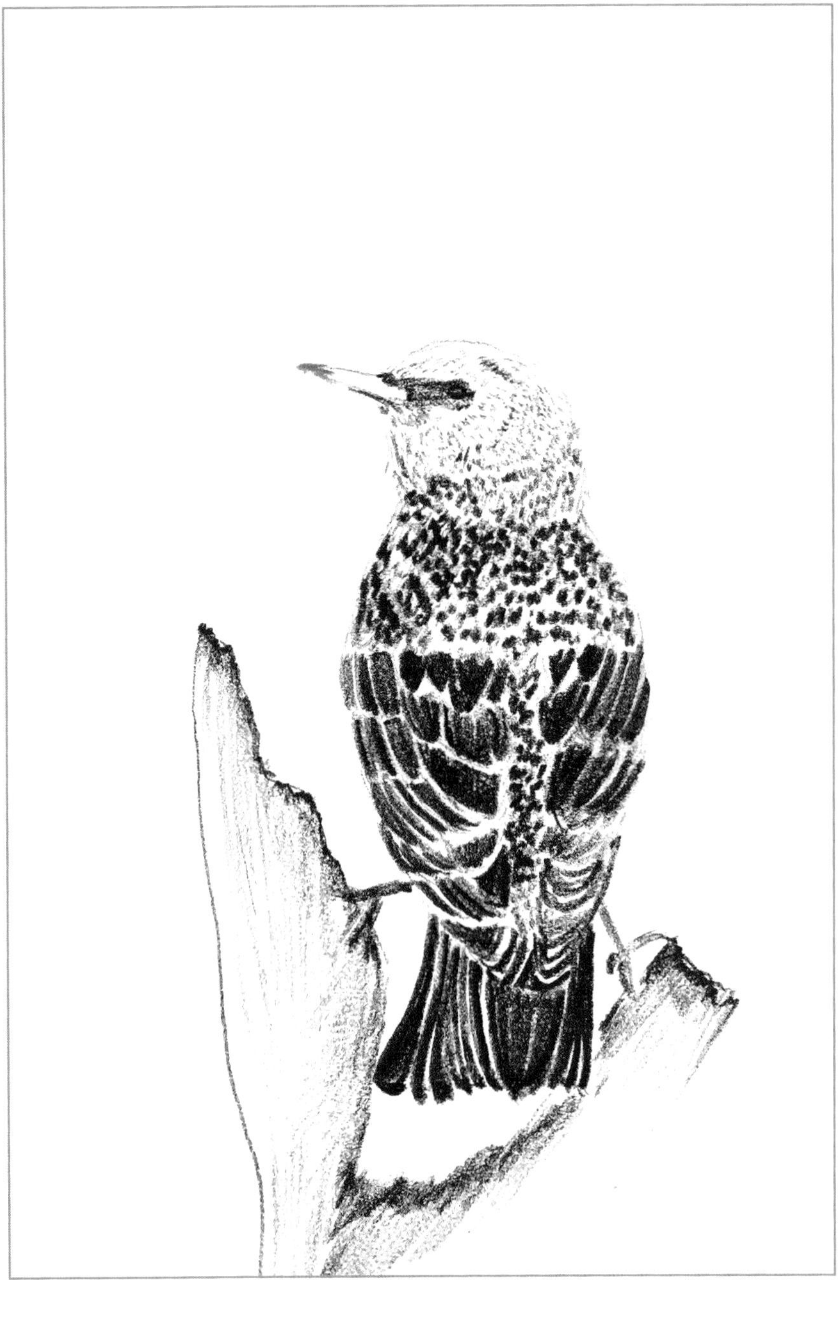

Starling

Drawn in pencil.

Hares

I drew these two, thinking of a couple celebrating Valentine's Day.

A gentleman bought the original drawing for his wife. He told me that the drawing reminded him of the very first time he met her. They were fortunate enough to spot a couple of hares bounding through the countryside.

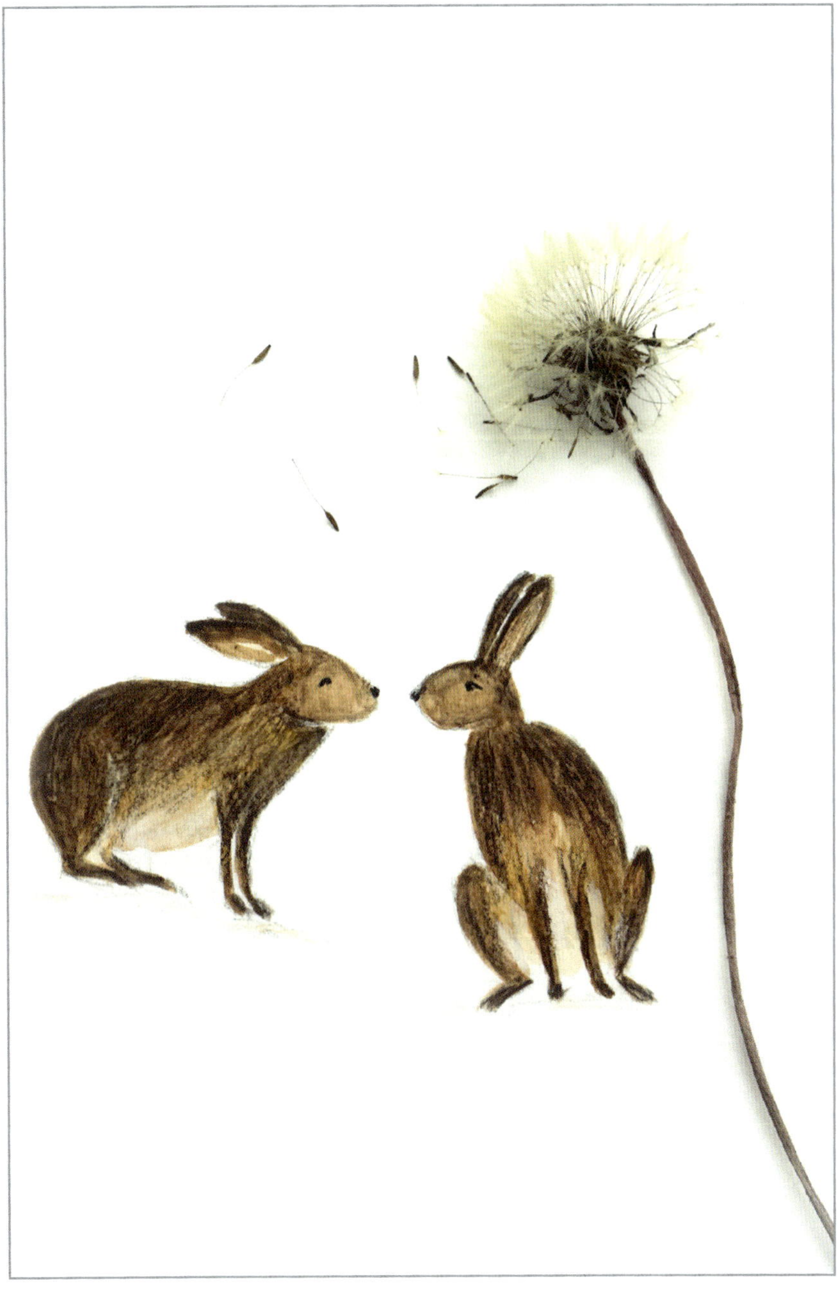

Lièvres Bruns

Painted with gouache. Finished with floating dandelion.

Baby Penguins

Baby penguins have lost their way.

The wind blows wild and by the icy white rock, these two are waiting for someone.

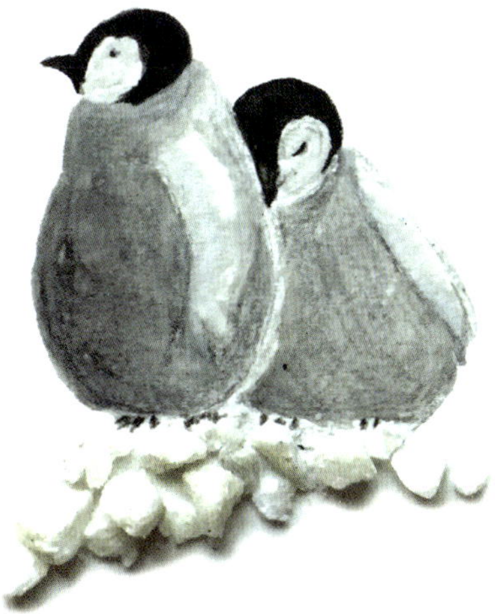

Baby Penguins

Painted with gouache. Finished with white stones.

Fox

It's always a bit of a surprise how my original drawing will end up. I rarely sketch out ideas beforehand and I pretty much never do more than one version, so each piece is unique.

For this drawing, it took me longer to adjust the snow effect than to create the actual drawing itself.

I waited for good sunlight to give me the perfect shadow on the snow, so that the natural shadow complemented the shadow I drew.

To the mountain

Painted with gouache. Finished with sea salt and fern.

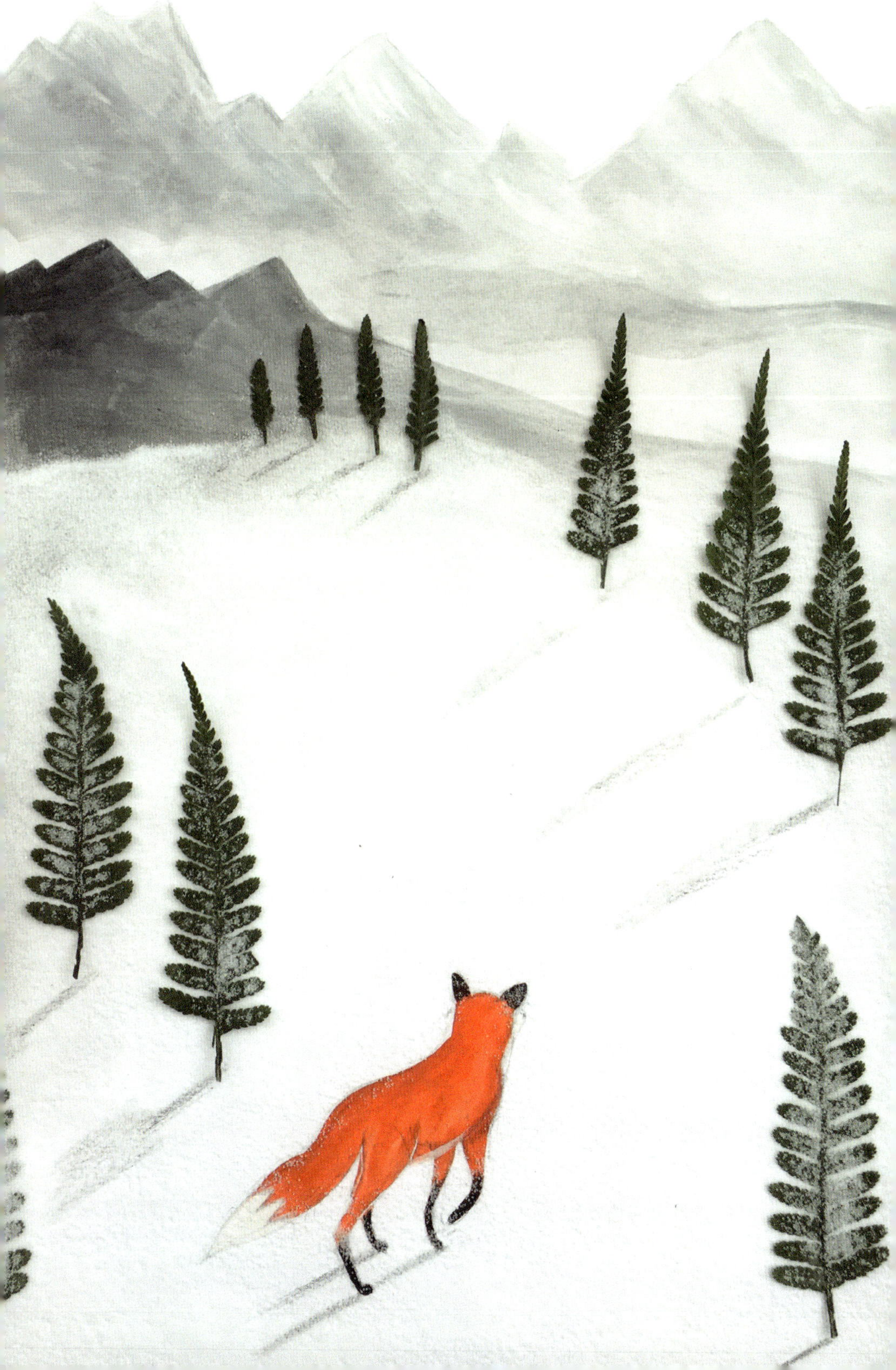

Penguins

Sometimes we have lots of cuddles and sometimes we might go a moment without cuddles, only to realise we want cuddles.

Can never have too many cuddles.

Especially when it's cold outside.

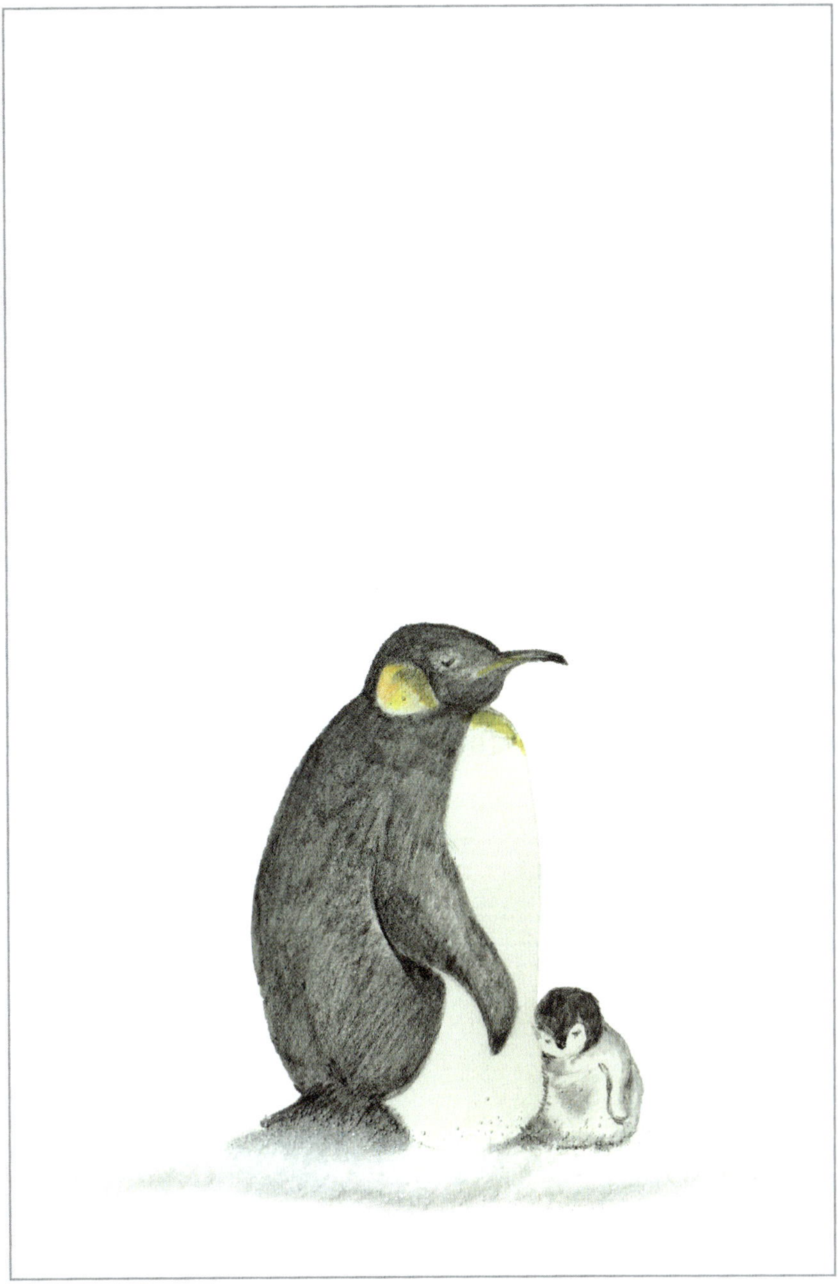

Cosy Christmas Cuddle

Drawn in pencil. Finished with sea salt.

Bears

Bear cub: Can I ask you something?

Big bear: Yes darling, of course.

Bear cub: How many days until Christmas?

Big bear: One less than I told you yesterday.

Bear cub: But how m....

Big bear: 23 days. Left. Until. Christmas.

When does your little cub start counting down?

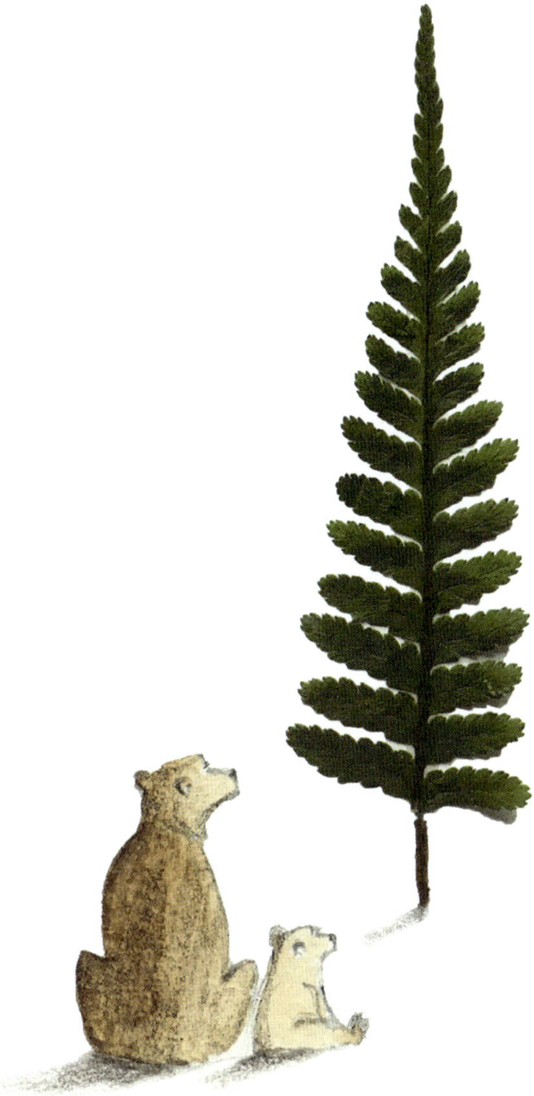

Bear and Cub

Painted with gouache. Finished with hand picked fern in Bath.

Robins

The festive season has begun.

Follow the robins...

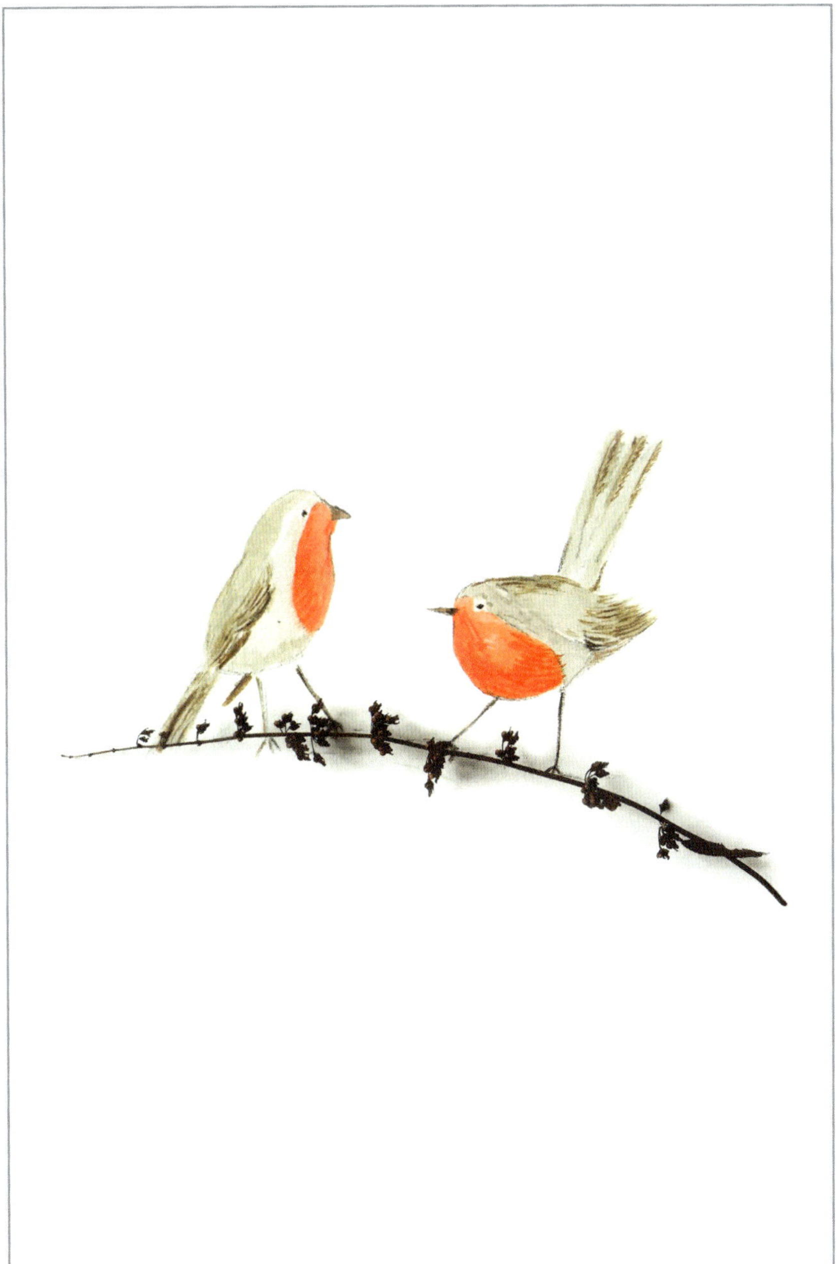

Robins

Painted with gouache. Finished with twig.

Through the window

One frosty morning, three little robins chirped upon a window sill.

Christmas day has begun, with all its warmth and festivities.

Through the window

Painted with gouache. Finished with sea salt.

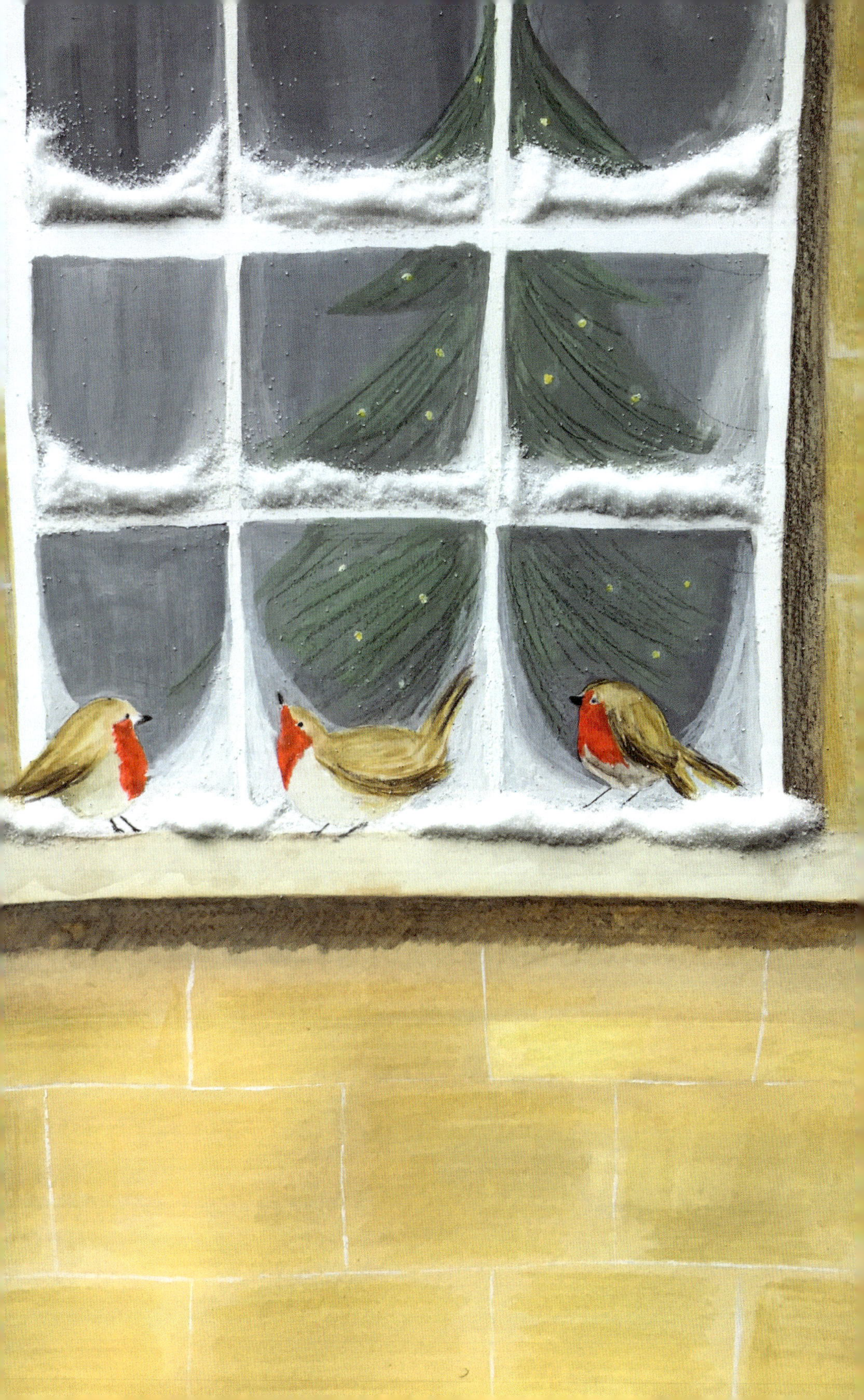

Deer

One early, warm summer morning in Bath, I was standing at my market stall in Queen Square, with a flask of coffee to perk me up. Just as I always have, I'd loaded the car the night before with my prints, greetings cards, framed originals, business cards and table, so that I could hit the road at sunrise.

Those of you who have ever traded at a market, trade fair (or even car boot to be honest!) know that you can never be quite sure how busy you will be. There had just been a few customers browsing that morning and barely a sale. Things weren't looking spectacular.

That can be a bitter pill to swallow, especially when you've put in a lot of preparation.

But then there are those moments that brighten the day completely. Something on my stall had caught the eye of a couple, riding past the square on their bikes. They pulled in, parked up and headed over.

The reindeer was the object of their attention.
"That's amazing. I'd love to have that on the front cover of the winter edition of my magazine" said the friendly gentleman, as he enthusiastically reached for a business card.

My day changed there and then... and the year finished very well indeed...

NB magazine

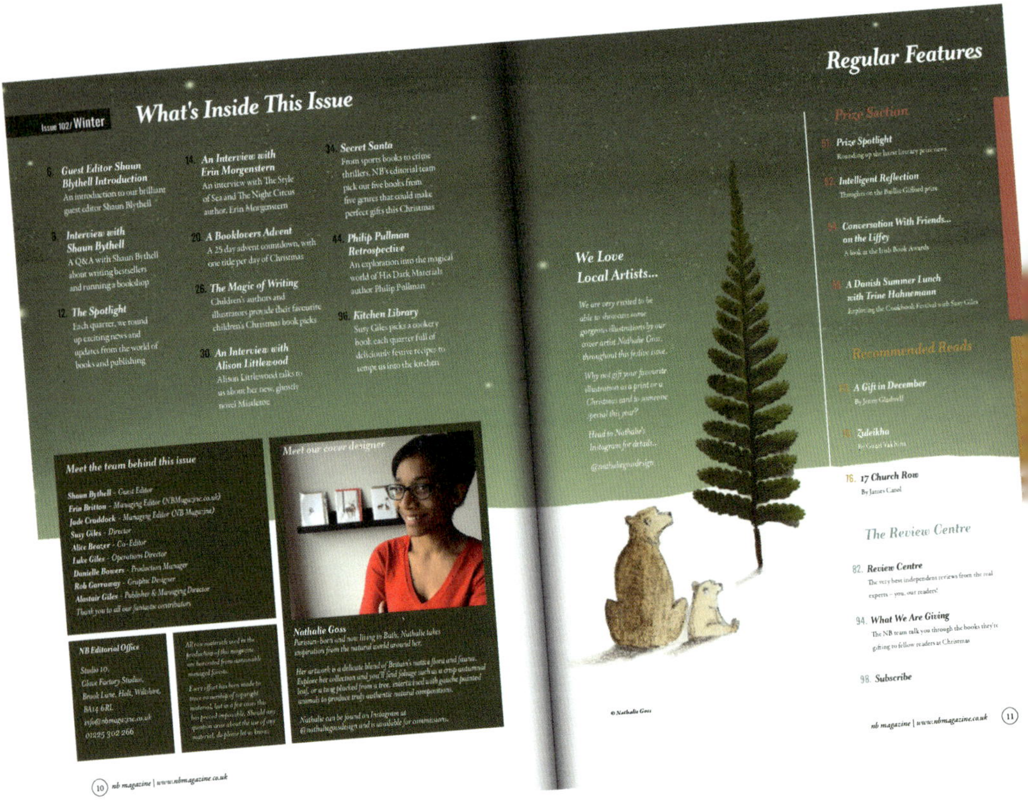

Issue 102/ Winter

What's Inside This Issue

Meet the team behind this issue

Shaun Bythell - *Guest Editor*
Erin Britton - *Managing Editor (NBMagazine.co.uk)*
Jade Craddock - *Managing Editor (NB Magazine)*
Susy Giles - *Director*
Alice Beazer - *Co-Editor*
Luke Giles - *Operations Director*
Danielle Bowers - *Production Manager*
Rob Garraway - *Graphic Designer*
Alastair Giles - *Publisher & Managing Director*
Thank you to all our fantastic contributors

NB Editorial Office

*Studio 10,
Glove Factory Studios,
Brook Lane, Holt, Wiltshire,
BA14 6RL
info@nbmagazine.co.uk
01225 302 266*

All raw materials used in the production of this magazine are harvested from sustainable managed forests.

Every effort has been made to trace ownership of copyright material, but in a few cases this has proved impossible. Should any question arise about the use of any material, do please let us know.

Meet our cover designer

Nathalie Goss
Parisian-born and now living in Bath, Nathalie takes inspiration from the natural world around her.

Her artwork is a delicate blend of Britain's native flora and fauna. Explore her collection and you'll find foliage such as a crisp autumnal leaf, or a twig plucked from a tree, intertwined with gouache painted animals to produce truly authentic natural compositions.

Nathalie can be found on Instagram at @nathaliegossdesign and is available for commissions.

We Love Local Artists...

We are very excited to be able to showcase some gorgeous illustrations by our cover artist Nathalie Goss, throughout this festive issue.

Why not gift your favourite illustration as a print or a Christmas card to someone special this year?

Head to Nathalie's Instagram for details...

@nathaliegossdesign

Regular Features

Prize Section

Recommended Reads

The Review Centre

© Nathalie Goss

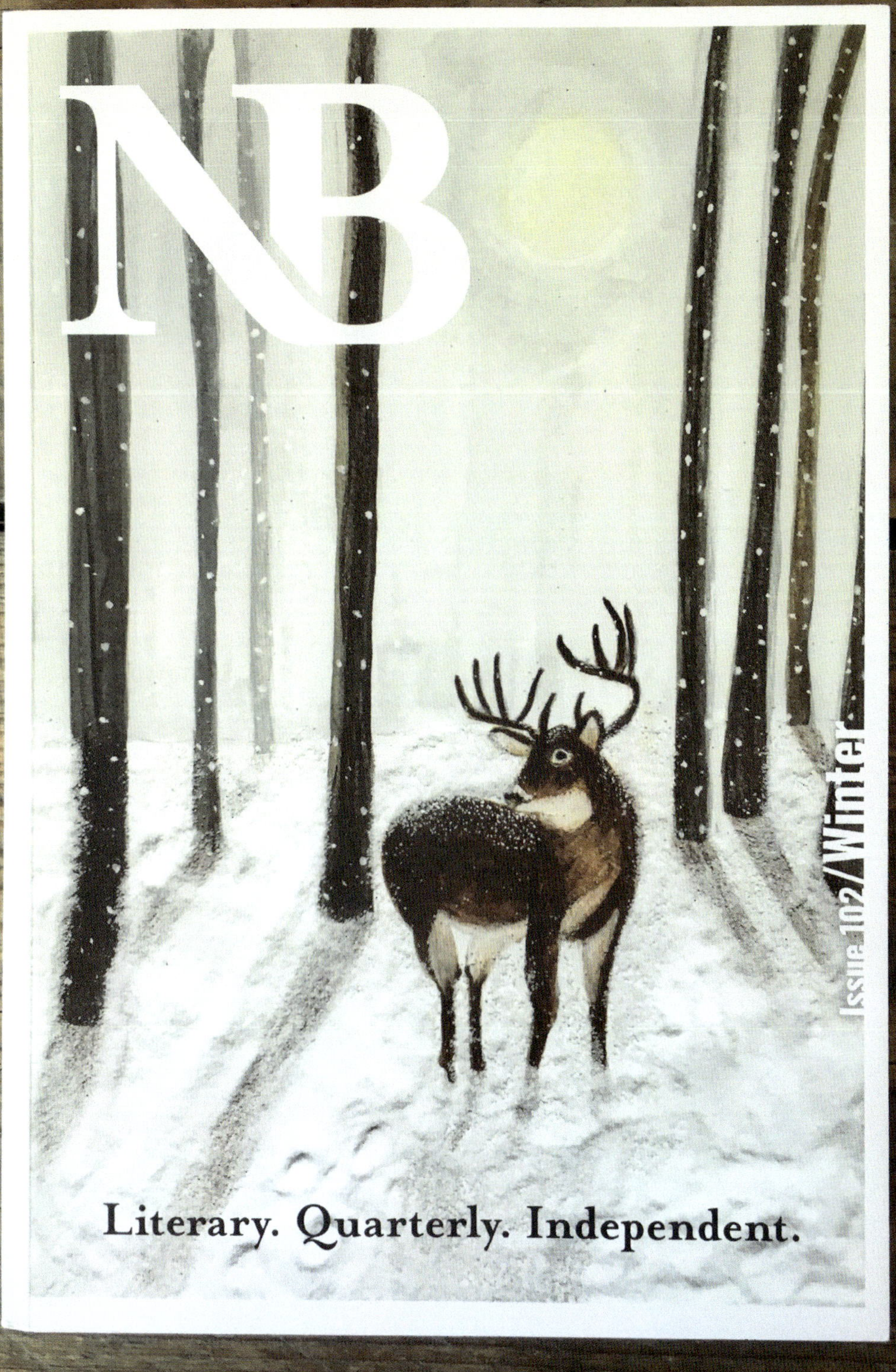
NB
Issue 102/Winter
Literary. Quarterly. Independent.

Beyond the ink

Here are some photographs of things I've been working on, including my bilingual children's book (Three Little Pigs / Trois Petits Cochons) and various other sketches...

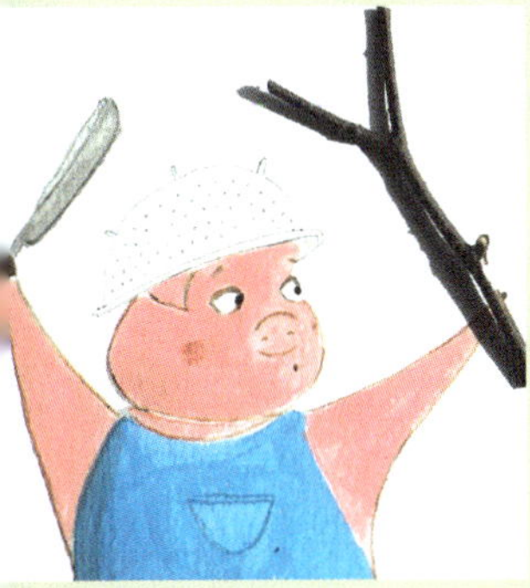
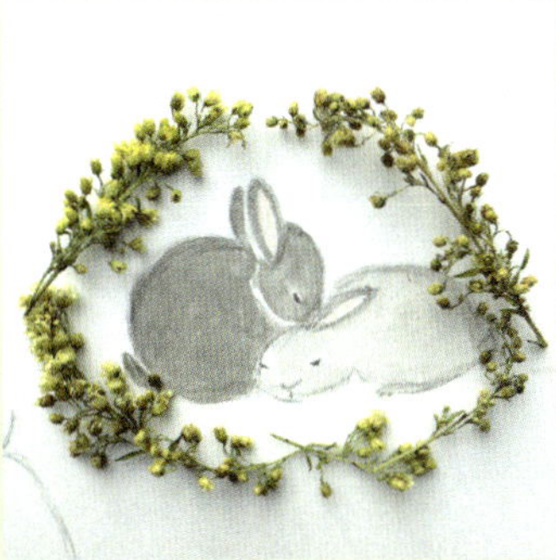
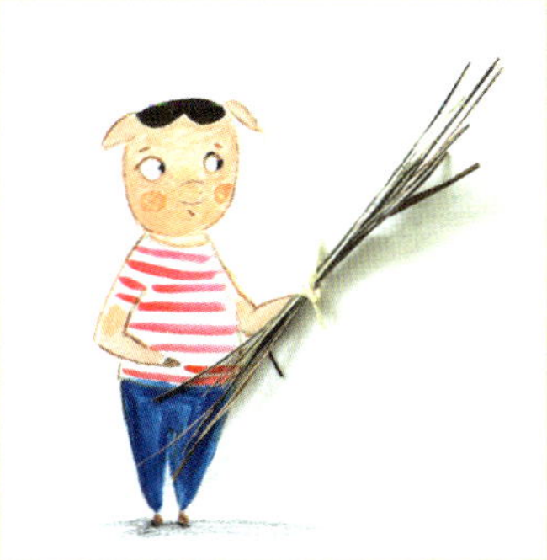
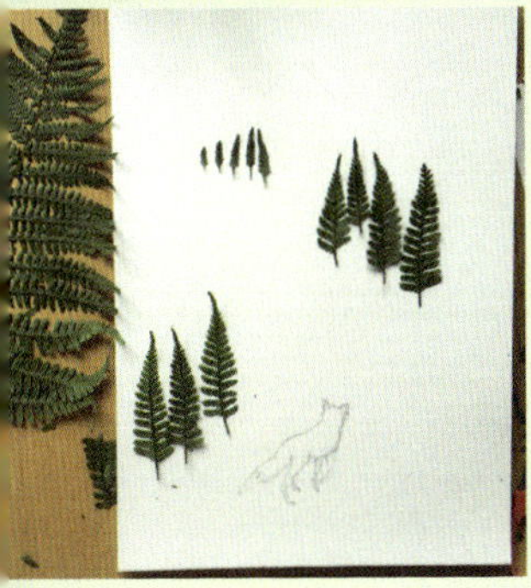
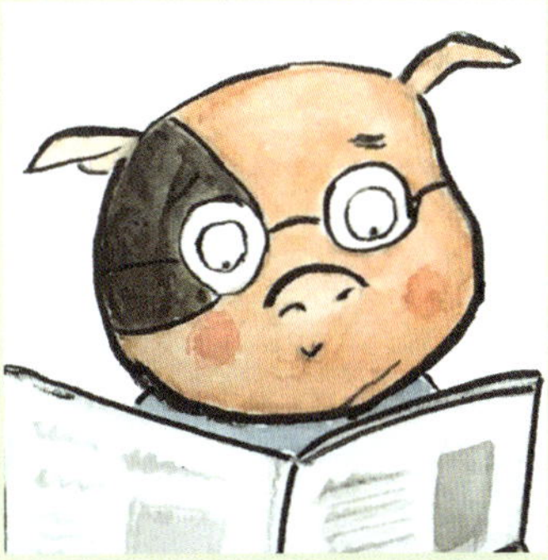
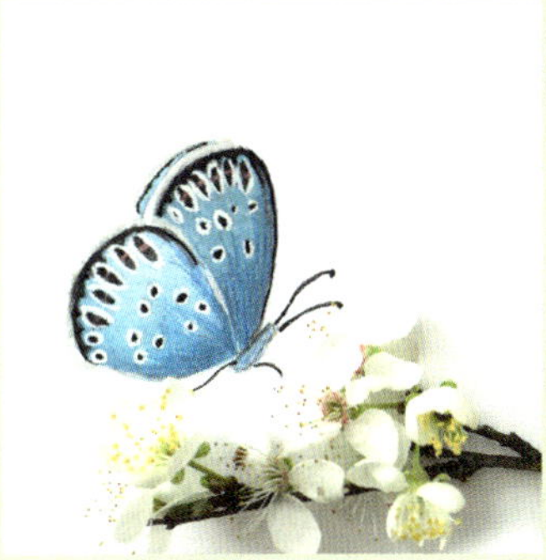

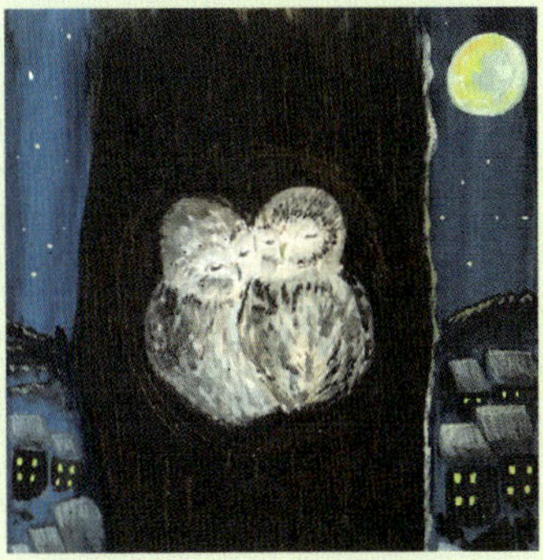
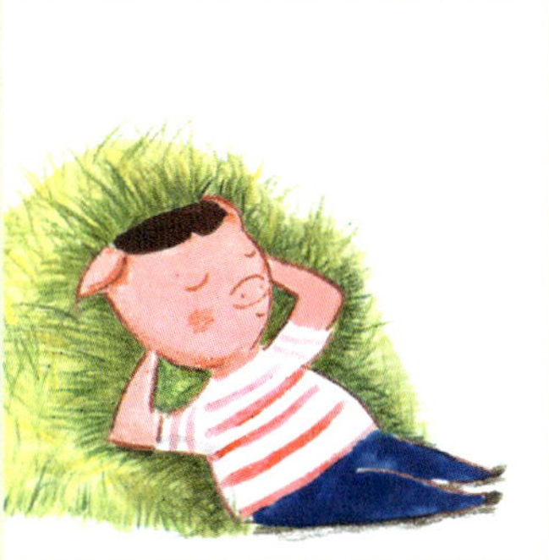
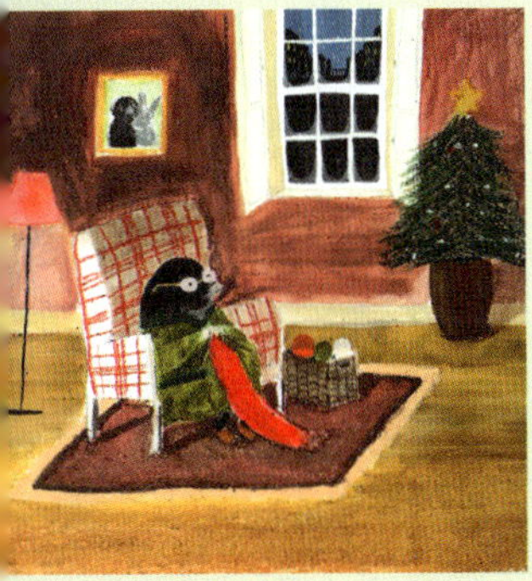
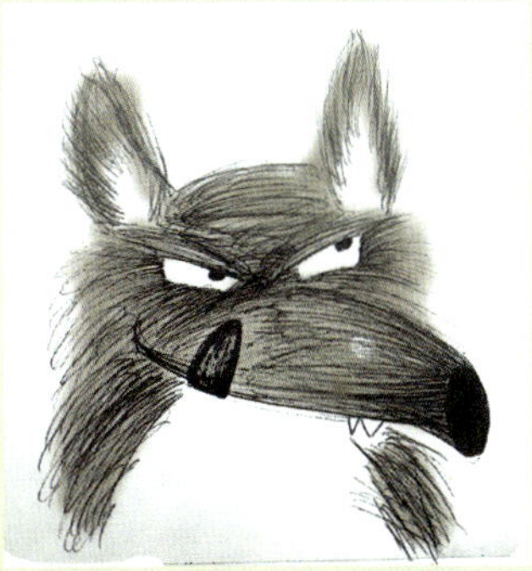
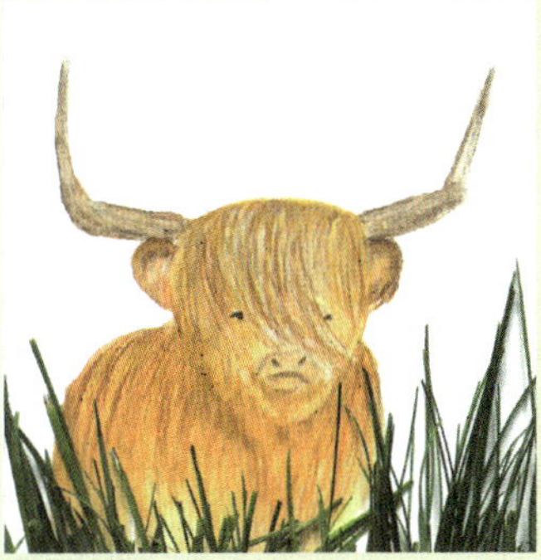

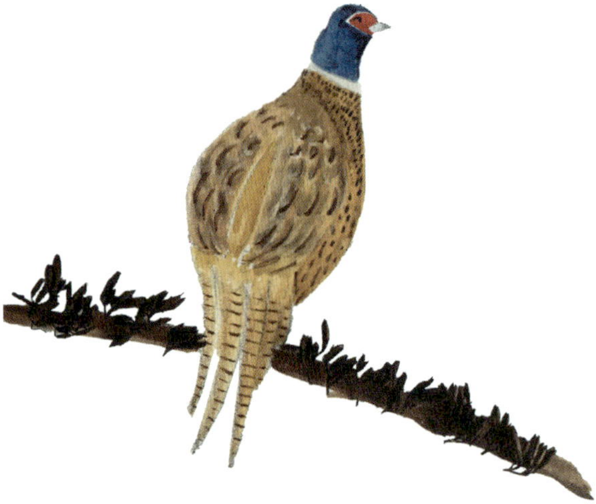

Thank you

A big thanks to you for reading my book and supporting me through my journey.

You can keep up to date with what I'm drawing on

Instagram: @nathaliegossdesigns

Facebook: Nathalie Goss

If you've enjoyed my work, please consider leaving a review of this book on Amazon.

Nathalie

x

Printed in Great Britain
by Amazon

63043655R00030

LO… …CK

A hilarious look at Potteries life past and present...

...with a Pottersaurus update!

Terry Bossons

JOLLEES

Forward

This book is...

...the follow up to "Book not Buck" and "Cook not Cuck"!

What can I call the next one?!???

A CIP catalogue record for this book is available from the British Library
ISBN 978-0-9929769-6-5

The Comedians!

12 amazing comedians and double acts who have graced the stage here in the Potteries. Were you lucky enough to attend one of these shows?

- **Ken Dodd** - Christmas happiness show - Victoria Hall, Hanley - most years
- **Tommy Cooper** - Jollees, Longton - January 1976
- **Billy Connolly** - Theatre Royal, Hanley - 6&7 September 1989

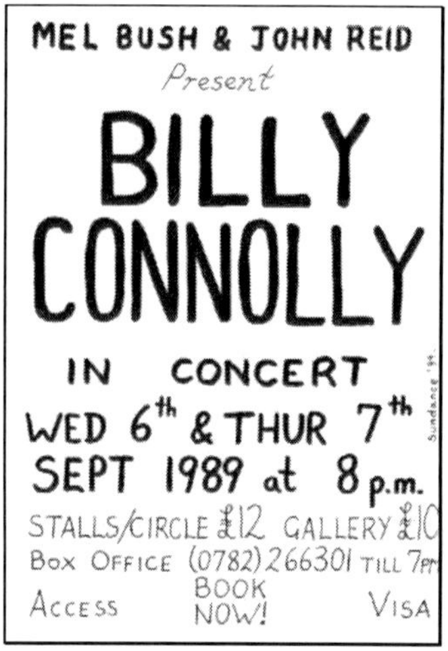

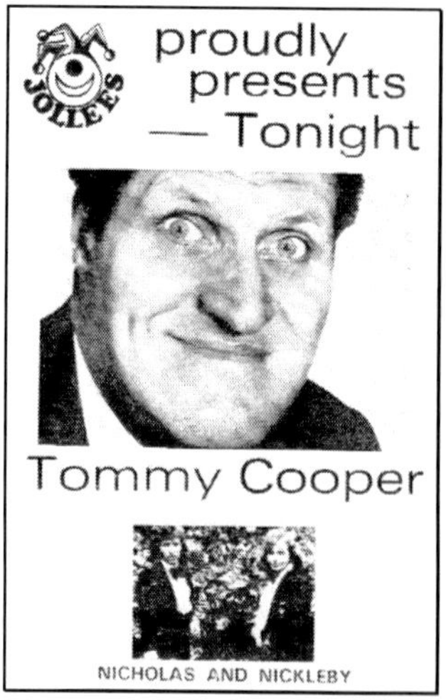

- **Peter Kay** - Mum Wants A Bungalow tour - Victoria Hall, Hanley - 24th Sept and 8th & 21st October 2002
- **Steve Coogan** - Alan Partridge and Other Less Successful Characters - Victoria Hall, Hanley - 1st October 2008
- **Russell Brand** - RE:Birth tour - Victoria Hall, Hanley - 14th November 2017
- **Bob Monkhouse** - Jollees, Longton - 15th - 18th June 1977

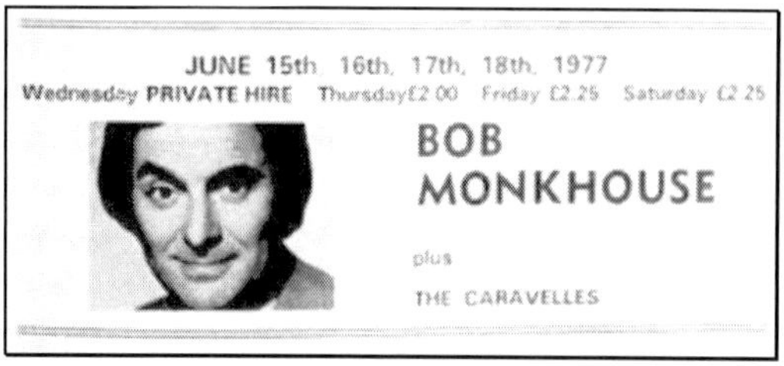

- **Joan Rivers** - Before the Doctor Pulls the Plug tour - Victoria Hall, Hanley - 24th October 2005
- **Micky Flanagan** (warm up for An' Another Fing tour) - Victoria Hall, Hanley - 28th January 2017
- **Chubby Brown** - Victoria Hall, Hanley - near enough every December
- **Morecambe and Wise** - Jollees, Longton- October 1976
- **Laurel and Hardy** - Theatre Royal, Hanley - March 21st 1952

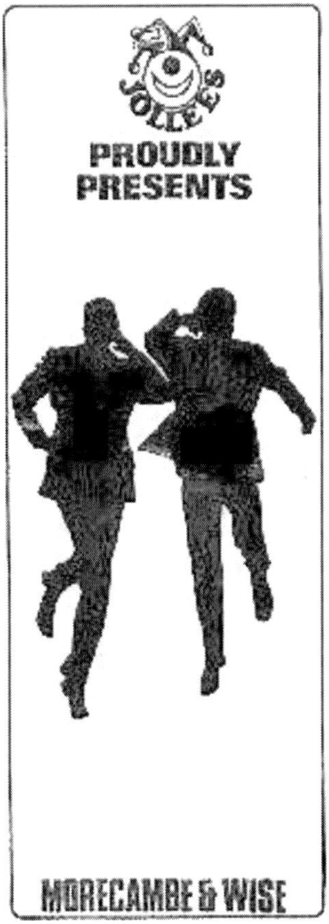

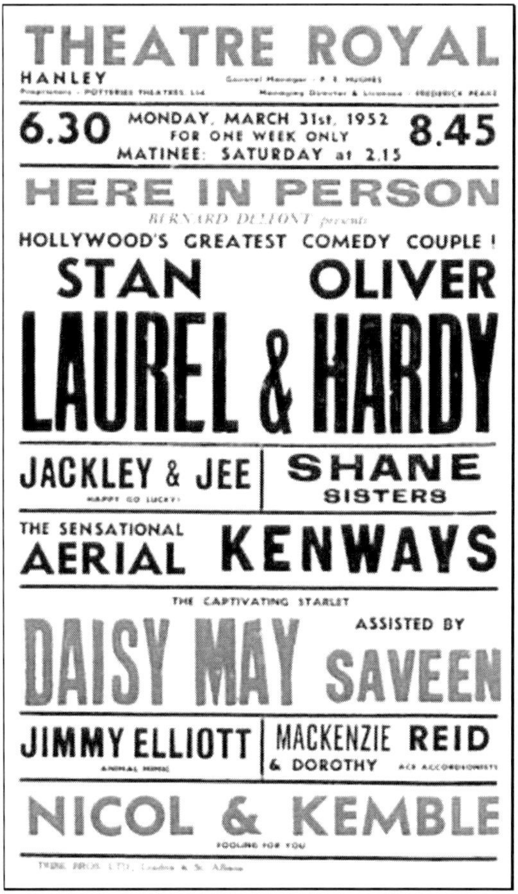

The Grumbleweeds

Robin Colvill from The Grumbleweeds has appeared in Stoke a few times over the years. Here he tells us about a gift he received after playing here in the 70s.

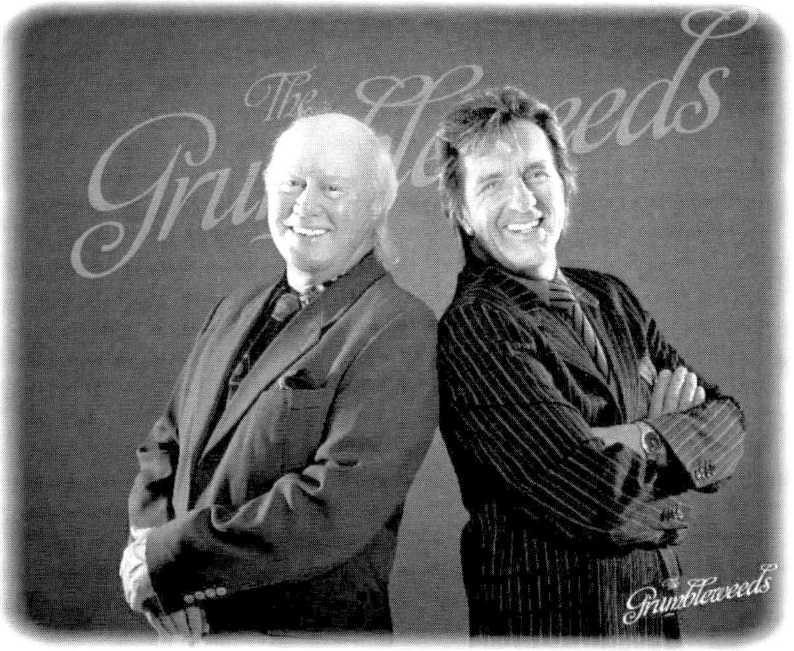

"We played the club above the bus station many times, Jollees. After making them a lot of money over the years, the owner took the 5 of us to Portmeirion pottery for a tour. At the end they gave us all a full set of Botanical gardens pottery, cups saucers, bowls, servers, jugs, plates; the box was huge. I kept this safe for 25 years only using it for "best". When I divorced in 2000 neither of us really wanted the stuff or had room for it with downsizing so it was agreed to sell it and split the money. Turns out it was all seconds and totally worthless, it would have been smashed up if it had not been given to us as presents!

Hey ho that's life! Robin x"

The Stoke Olympics

Trent Vale Poet
(1960 - 2018)

The oatcake and the Sentinel
Meet at Radio Stoke
And Robbie Williams' fayther
That old Pete Conway bloke
Sings to us Delilah
As outside pubs we smoke
Cos that's what's bin decided
By them down in the smoke
The mayor's a nightmare
He dunner have a clue
If I had ten bob spare duck
I'd waste it all upon you
Me sweet Cultured Quarter
In a desert of decline
Where the potbanks have been slaughtered
And the buses dunner run on time
Football, give us football
Win, lose or draw
Eat yourself up inside out
Go back for more
We know nothing worth knowing
Knowing it is not
Be thankful for small mercies
Cherish what you've got
Traffic's at a standstill
I'm on my last legs
Amongst the dregs of society
Most of whom are close friends
An ill-founded reputation
The butt of many a joke
We're not as bad as painted though
I'm proud to say I come from Stoke

I WAS BORN IN STOKE-ON-TRENT

Merrym'n

I've heard about the singing pig,
Up the road from where me great uncle lived,
I've met the ghost at The Leopard kid,
Led me up the wooden hills to the room she still kept,

Heard many a tall tale,
Through that broken old accent,
Yeah, I was born in Stoke-on-Trent.

I don't know much, that's for sure,
But I know what's knocking at my front door,
I remember the wheels of the colliery,
Watched them turn away into history,

And I've been told time and again,
As I'm tucked into bed,
Yeah, I was born in Stoke-on-Trent.

You may think of fierce looking women,
You may think of drunken old fools,
Pinching a living,
Propped up in old school shoes.

But I think about the wizard of the wing,
And how he'd twist and turn and make them sing...
I think of a glorious past,
As I walk on down the Caldon canal,

I think of my roots,
And how they're heaven sent,
Yeah, I was born in Stoke-on-Trent.

Jimmy Cricket

"It's Jimmy, come closer but stay 2 metres away!

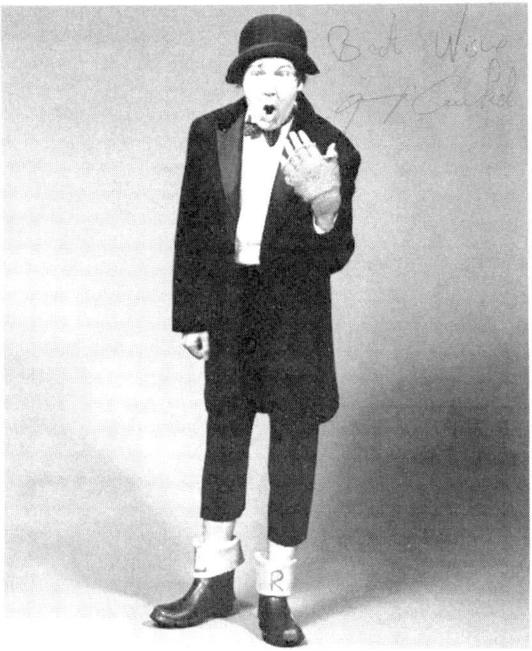

Jimmy Cricket

"I used to love working the Potteries. They were always warm hearted and enthusiastic audiences. I remember I did a place called Trentham Gardens several times.

"The fee would always be the same - £25 - and sometimes they'd get you to do an extra spot in the upstairs function room. I also did the Olympic Club and then the biggie – Jollees!

"I supported The Stylistics for a week, and there was a compere called Mel Scholes who was good fun.

"The typical type of joke I did back then was 'Ladies and gentlemen, come'ere, I went fishing to-day and I fell in. A fella jumped in and pulled me out. He said "How did you come to fall in?" I said "I didn't come to fall in, I came to fish!"'

Stay healthy, Jimmy Cricket"

Jokecakes

To celebrate 10 years of Oatcake Day in 2020, here are 10 jokecakes:

What did cavemen have on their oatcakes?
Dinosauce

What's bacons favourite day?
Fry day

What time do oatcakes rise?
When you yeast expect them to

What's an oatcakes favourite soul singer?
Toni Baxton

Where do AC/DC get their oatcakes?
On High Lane near Chell

Why did the oatcake go to the dentist?
It needed a filling

What's better than a good friend?
A good friend with oatcakes

Knock knock
Who's there
Annie
Annie who
Annie get ya oatcakes, get ya oatcakes Annie

What's green and smells like bacon?
Kermit's fingers (after eating an oatcake)

One more oatcake joke? Nahhh, it's way too cheesy!

Names you hardly see

When naming children, parents hunt high and low for a cool name for their offspring. The biggest Christian names at the moment are 'Luna' for a girl and 'Asher' for a boy. Here is a list of old fashioned names, Will Amy of these make a comeback?!?

Ada
Alan
Albert
Alec
Alfred
Anne
Arnold
Barbara
Barney
Barry
Basil
Brenda
Charles
Clement
Cuthbert
Deirdre
Doreen
Doris
Douglas
Duncan
Edna
Eli
Elizabeth
Elsie
Enid
Ernie
Ethel
Eric
Frank
Fred
Freda
Gertie
Gladys
Glennis
Gordon
Gwen
Gwyneth
Harold
Hazel
Herbert
Hilda
Ida
Janice
Jean
Jemima
Joseph
Josiah
Joyce
Keith
Kenneth
Kevin
Lettice
Madge
Maud
Maureen
Moira
Nellie
Nora
Norbert
Noreen
Norma
Norris
Olive
Olwyn
Pamela
Pauline
Peter
Ralf
Reginald
Roger
Roland
Samuel
Stanley
Timothy
Una
Vera
Vincent
Victor

Potteries guide to Covid-19

STAY AT WOM

PROTEC TH' NHS DUCK

SAVE LARVES

- **Co feed narntane** - Covid-19
- **Pondemick** - Pandemic
- **Quorantane** - Quarantine
- **Sell fice layshun** - Self isolation
- **Wesh thar onds (or wash thee onds)** - Wash your hands
- **Toe mater rool** - Two metre rule
- **Croner virus** - Coronavirus
- **Feece mosk** - Face mask
- **Fir load** - Furloughed
- **Kayp thee distance** - Keep your distance
- **So shall distunce** - Social distance
- **Sing oppy bothdee twace** - Sing Happy Birthday twice
- **Dunner goo ite** - Don't go out
- **Osspittle** - Hospital
- **Nosses** - Nurses
- **Are conner braythe rate** - I can't breathe properly
- **Vackseen** - Vaccine
- **Omblunce** - Ambulance

Lockdown jokes

During this lockdown Robbie Williams has been doing an Open University course on Trigonometry.

...

So through it all....he's loving angle's instead!!

I phoned B&Q during lockdown and said "How big is the queue?"

...

The bloke who answered thought for a second and replied "Same size as the B!"

What's the difference between COVID-19 and Romeo and Juliet?

...

One's the coronavirus and the other is a Verona crisis.

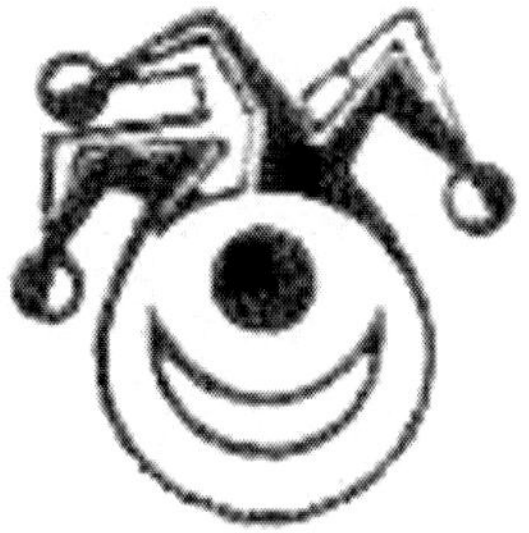

Mel Scholes

Mel Scholes by Terry Bossons

Queuing in the rain
Beneath coats and brollies
They lined up in their scores
To be entertained at Jollees

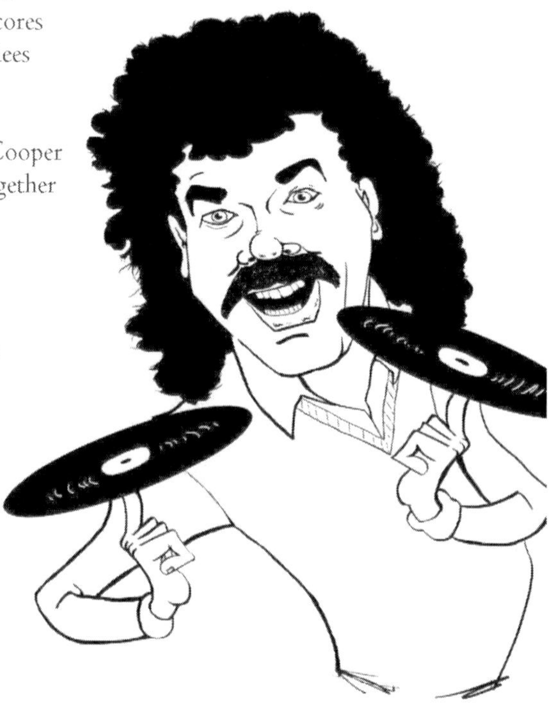

To see Little and Large
And the great Tommy Cooper
The man who held it together
Was no party pooper

His name was Mel
Second names Scholes
Laughter and merriment
Were two of his goals

In dapper suits
With one line jokes
On stage and radio
He entertained us folks

From the end of Neck
To the end of Bignall
We had our wirelesses
Tuned in to Signal

With a 'rat tee tat'
And an 'Up 'Anley duck'
Scholesy informed us
It was book not buck!

He's no longer here
Oh how time flies
He's upstairs on stage
Entertaining the skies

Cannon and Ball

Cannon and Ball by Terry Bossons

With a massive grin
In The Viccy Hall
I was ten years old
Watching Cannon and Ball

They came on stage
As we took our places
I really wanted to twang
Bobby Ball's braces.

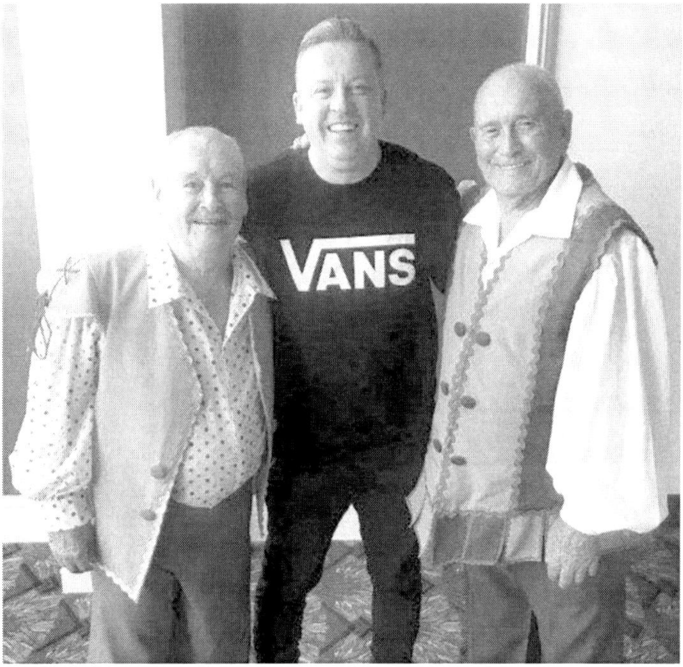

It was my first live show
With pocket money saved
I thought it was at me
When Tom and Bobby waved

The hour flew by
Before we had to go home
I bought a signed photo
And a "Rock on Tommy" comb

They still make me laugh
It takes me back to that day
Their song has a message
Cos "Together, we'll be ok"

The Potters Fortnight

Remember the good old Potters fortnight? The last week of June and the first week of July, Potbanks, factories and schools in Stoke had their annual holiday. The six town centres were deserted as many folks headed to the seaside.

PMT double deckers and WMC organised coaches would ship families for a day trip to Blackpool, Rhyl, Towyn and other beaches. If you were lucky it would be a week there if your parents had done well during 'bull week' and brought home a few extra quid. Sometimes you would bump into people you knew at the seaside because foreign holidays were for the well off.

If you had a Stoke-cation and stayed at home, it was playing out till it went dark. It usually rained and we would be stuck in some days watching Wimbledon on the TV.

Pat Collins

The Pat Collins fair came to town up Hanley, some of us went on the bus to try and win a goldfish and have a go on the Waltzer. The circus also came to Hanley Park which made a great day out.

The Potters holiday tradition has now disappeared due to the decline of Pottery industry and schools objecting to the holidays at crucial exam times. But those who remember them will look back with a smile.

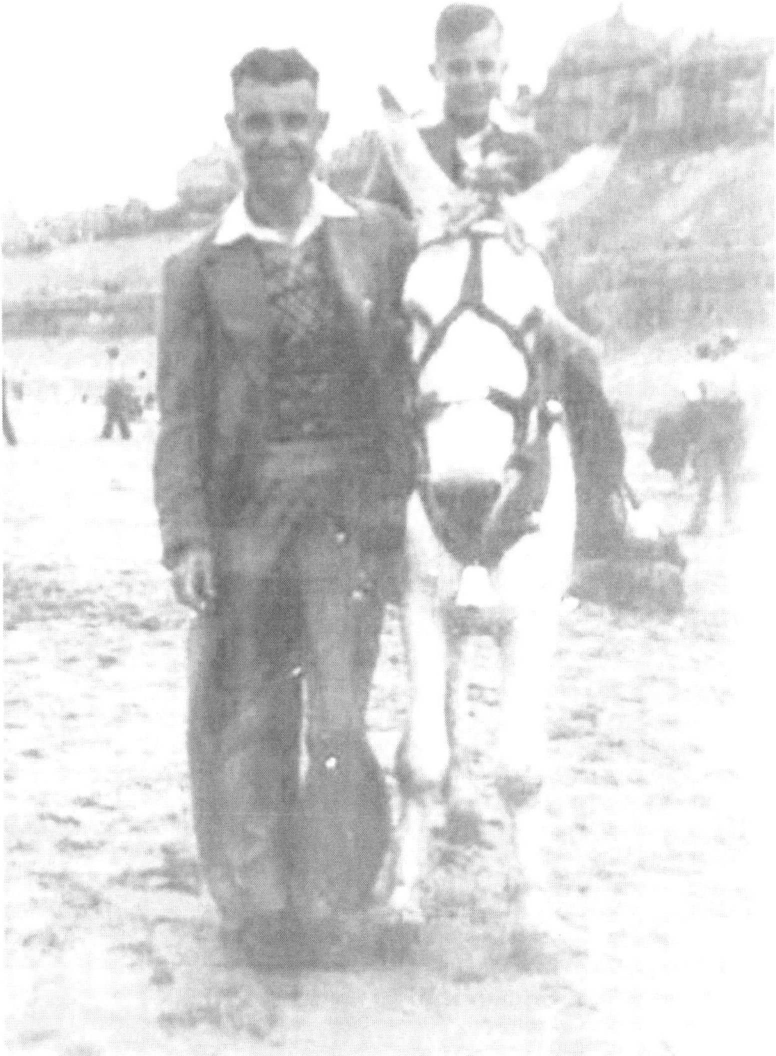

Phil McGraw riding a donkey with his dad on North Beach, Blackpool during the Potters fortnight in the late 1940s

Stan Boardman

The legendary Liverpudlian comedian loves the Potteries and one place is always in his heart. He still has a pile of photographs that were taken off the walls of Jollees when they had a refurb.

I had a chat to him during lockdown to find out why Stoke holds some great memories...

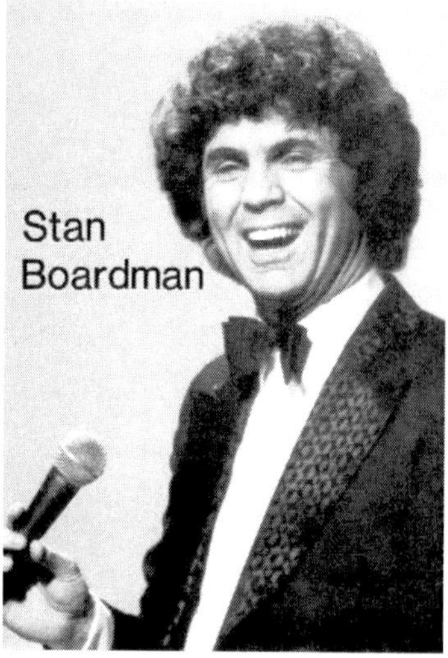

"I loved Jollees but getting there was the hardest part, finding the bloody place. I jumped out of the car because in them days you didn't have a mobile phone so I rang up the club.
I said "I can't find you, I'm all over the Potteries".
Mike Massey the manager said "Follow the number 74 bus".
I said "Why's that?"
Mike said "Because we're in the bus station!"

It was a fantastic club and the compere, Mel Scholes made you feel at ease. There was a lamp on every table and you could watch Shirley Bassey whilst eating chicken in a basket. If you hadn't got enough money it was scampi in a hanky.

I remember doing a good show there and when I came off there was about forty people outside the dressing room door wanting autographs. When I came out I was signing, signing and signing for about half an hour. When it got to the very last fella, he come up to me and said "You were sh*t!". He had queued up for thirty minutes to tell me.

I played round Burslem a lot too, in the working men's clubs. Stoke was always great to play as it had twenty clubs in a twenty mile radius.

One time I was working at a hotel and the Stoke player Adrian Heath had just transferred to Everton. He came in whilst I was on stage wearing a white jacket. Everyone clapped so I stopped my act and said "You've just signed for Everton?" and he said yes. I said "Don't go round Liverpool wearing that jacket, people will think you are selling cockles and muscles".

Bully!

You can't beat a bit of bully!

Pete Conway was at a quiet service station with darts legend, Phil 'The Power' Taylor a few years back having a coffee.

A woman working at the service station comes up to Phil and says:
"You do make me laugh!"

Phil replies: "Make you laugh?"

Woman replies: "You're Peter Kay aren't you?"

Co worker says: "Nooooo, It's the darts player!"

Woman says: "Can I have your autograph anyway?"

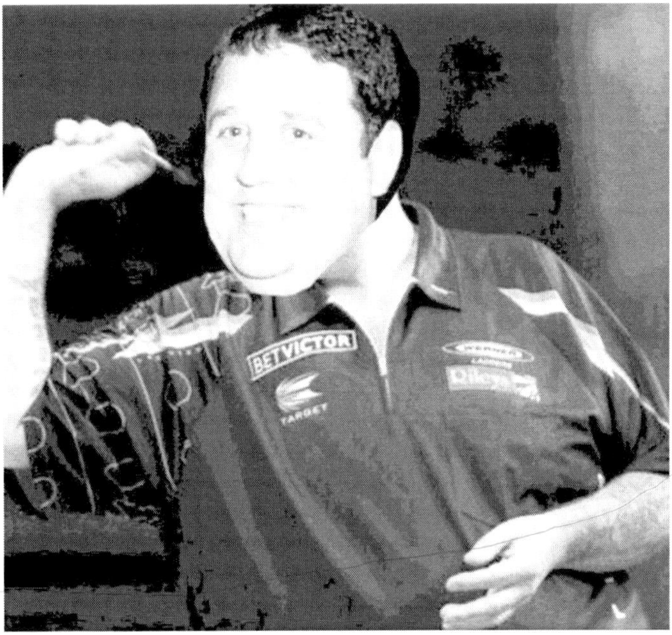

Haircut 100

In 2020, Lockdown had us cutting our own hair through necessity but back in the day our barnets weren't DIY but DBM (done by mum).

Mums would get out the big pudding bowl and the kitchen scissors and give us a quick trim the night before the school photos were being taken. We would pray for at least a straight line but it rarely happened.

A few locals have shared their horror haircuts.

Simon Lindop

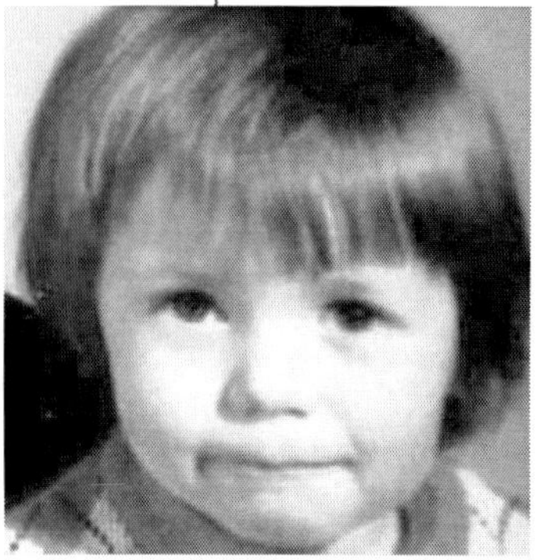

Neil Hood

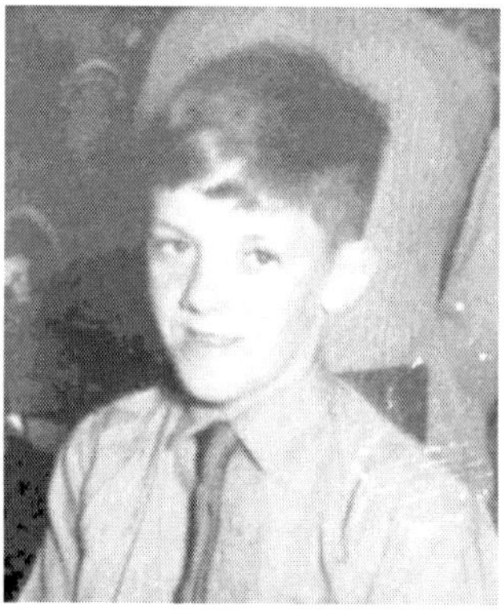

Alan May

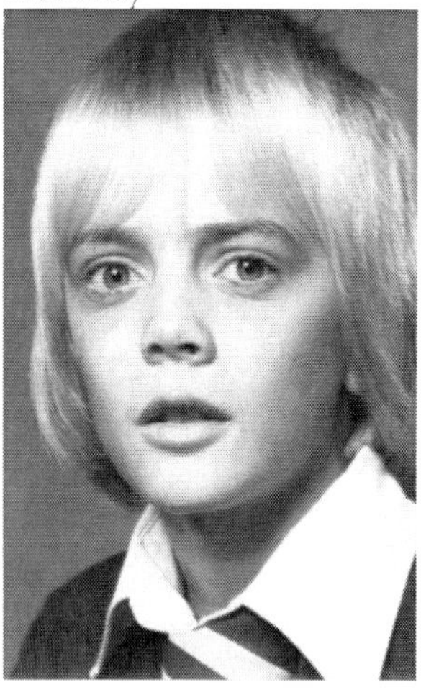

Darren Anstey.

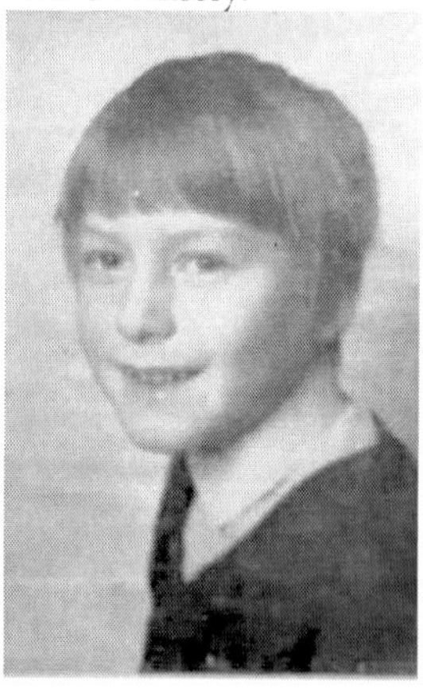

Gary Ellerton

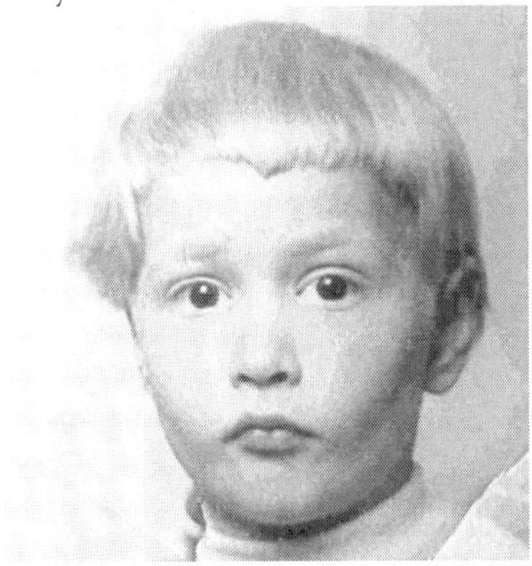

Gail Peters and her brother.

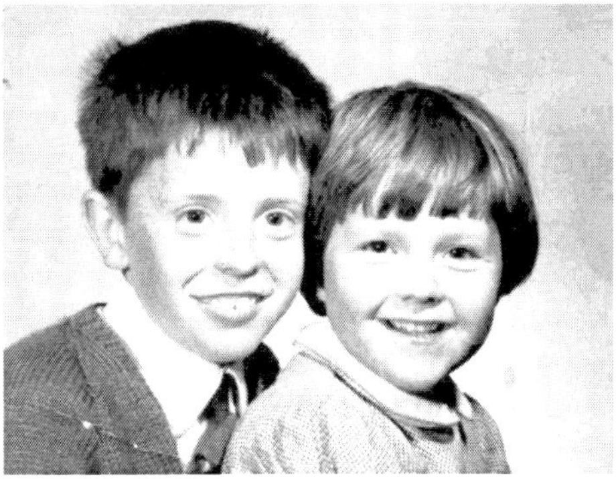

Terry Bossons

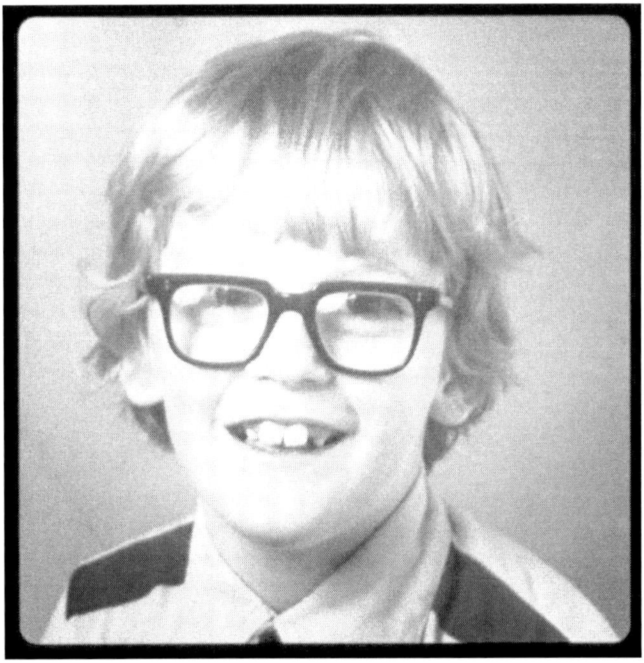

Singalong to Angels

Let's have a Staffordshire sing-a-long....to the tune of Robbie's "Angels":

Chell **Sideway**
Dresden **Hanley**
Cheadle, **Baldwin's Gate.**

Hanford **Smallthorne**
Tean **Penkhull** Bucknall
Middleport **Kidsgrove**
Cross Heath **Sneyd** Stone
Leek **Stoke Station**
Longport **Ellastone**
Stanfields **Blurton** Newstead
Tunstall **Fenton** Loggerheads
Hartshill **Keele** Birches Head
Uttoxetter **Harriseahead**

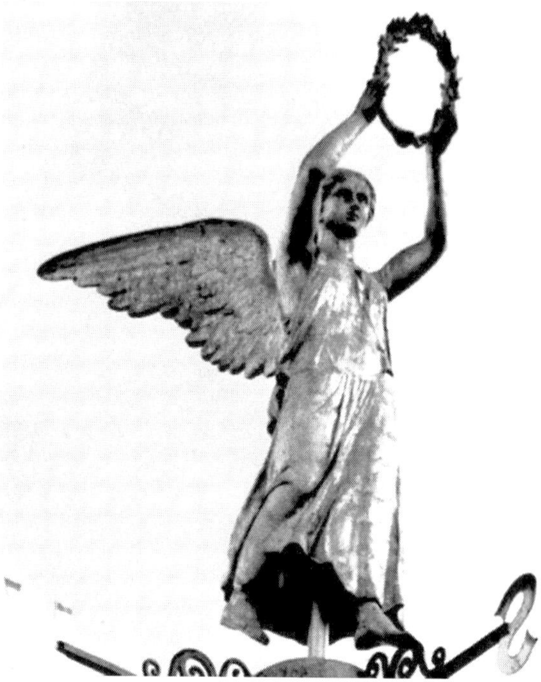

Etruria **Clough Hall**
Shelton **Alton** Talke **Fenton**
Bentilee **Biddulph** Longton
Werrington **Cheddleton**

Heron Cross **Park Hall**
Wolstanton **May Bank** Bradeley
Ipstones **Knypersley** Audley
Westlands **Eccleshall**
Trentham **Forsbrook** Meir
Uttoxeter **Harriseahead**

DJ Tales

When DJs and bar staff hear the boss say "The area manager is coming tonight!" it's all hands on deck to make sure the venue is rocking. This happens a lot, so about ten years ago I heard a brand new area manager was coming in so I upped my game accordingly.

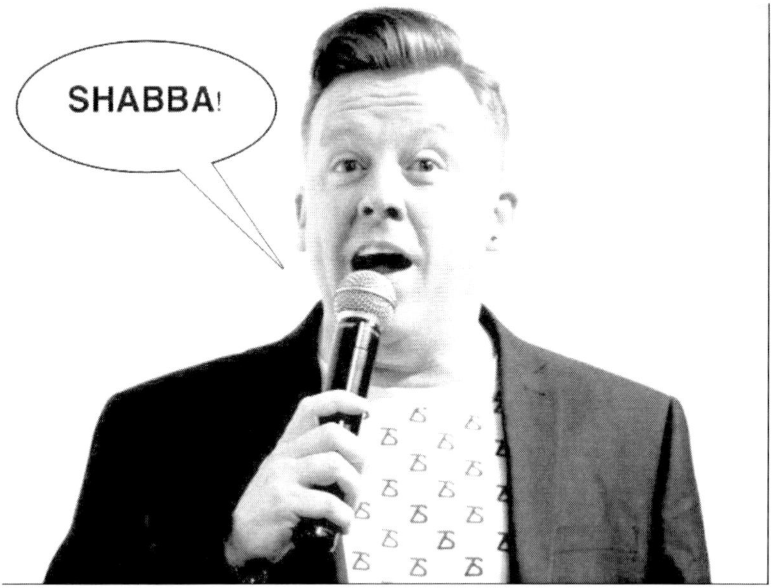

My boss said the new guy was in his fifties and as I was doing a student night I thought he would be easy to spot. So it's about ten o'clock and I spy a guy by the bar fitting the description. He heads over and says hello and shakes my hand and then asks for the most random songs ever. The students love retro and sing-a-long tunes but this guy's requests were leftfield and emptied the dancefloor.

This continued for about two hours before he finally drank up, waved and left the venue. With about one hour remaining of the night I saw my boss and shouted him over. I told him I had looked after the area manager and entertained his very odd music choices. My boss looked at me strangely and said "He hasn't been in, he called to say he would be in next week!" So I had made a random guy feel very special and probably ruined a lot of people's fun.

Terry Bossons

Slash remembers Stoke-on-Trent

Over the years working at 6 Towns Radio I have been lucky enough to become friends with some of Slash's family. This has meant a few meetings with the rock legend and we have had some good chats.

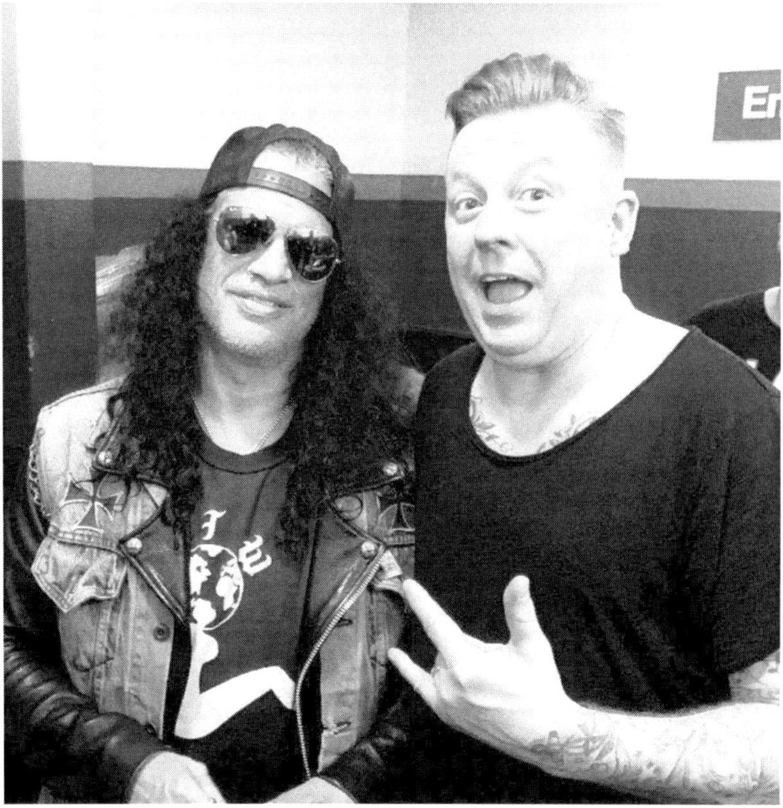

One time I asked him what he recalled about his years growing up in Stoke. My mind was thinking he would say pot banks, oatcakes of perhaps some of our amazing heritage.

He said "I remember riding a bus and it being very grey as it rained a lot."

I'm guessing we weren't in his mind set when he was writing "Paradise City" with Guns 'N' Roses.

Back in 2011, Slash made a return to the area and played the Viccy Hall in Hanley, I luckily became acquainted with his uncle around this time.

Ian Hudson helped look after a very young Slash and one day came down to 6 Towns Radio to chat about his famous nephew.

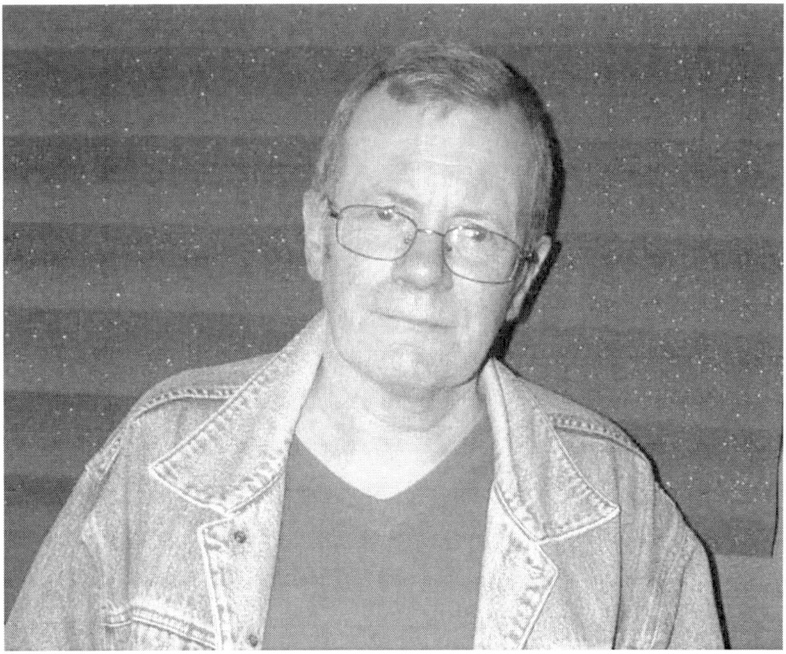

Uncle Ian is a quiet spoken, lovely man who's obviously very proud of Slash and what he has achieved. On my first meeting with Ian he told me a story that shows what a top bloke he is.

A few years ago, Ian was in a bar in Fenton waiting for a friend, a random stranger strikes up conversation with him. He says a few weird things to Ian who is wishing his friend would hurry up so he could get away. The bloke then turns to Ian and says "My only claim to fame is that I'm Slash's uncle". Ian just replied "oh, are you?" and left it at that, without letting on that he himself was related to the Guns N' Roses megastar.

I bet the guy dined our on that lie for a while but still doesn't know he said it to Slash's actual uncle!

Games

Before computer games, we had to make our own fun and with zero budget. Here are a few games that were played on the streets round here (proper sports not included).

Kerby.

You and a friend stand on opposite sides of the road and have to throw a ball at the opposite kerb. If you hit it and it bounces back then you get another shot from half way. You either played until one person reached ten points or kept going and the winner is the one with the highest score.

Tick.

One person is 'on' and an unlimited amount of people have to run off. If you are caught by the person who is 'on' and they say tick, then it's your turn to be 'on'

Off ground tick.

Another version of tick where you can be immune from being caught if both your feet are off the ground.

Red rover.

Two lines of similar number teams call over someone from the other team. Both lines are all joined hand to hand and if the person called over can't break the link they have to join your team. The winning team is the one with the most, if not all the players when the school bell went.

Stokie.

Two teams of equal numbers compete against each other. One team chases and the other team runs away. If one of the chasers catch a runner they say 'Stokie 123'. This goes on until all the runners are caught then the runners become the chasers. An alternative version has a 'base' where caught runners are held, these can be freed if tagged by other runners who evade the catchers.

British Bulldog.

Players have to run from one side of the playground to the other. One person is 'on' and if they catch a runner they too have to help catch the runners.

Hide and seek.

Self-explanatory really, one player or team hides whilst the others count to a certain number then seek. Then you change over.

Hopscotch .

A chalk pattern is drawn on the floor and you have to hop over it in a certain way.

Rallio.

Everyone stands with both hands on the wall and one person stands alone. They shout 'go' and everybody runs, if you got tagged then you are out. If you touched the wall again you could rest but you had to say "Rallio Rallio 123". This continues till everyone is caught.

Hedgehopping.

Basically it's vaulting over people hedges and fences.

Knock a door run.

You dare someone to knock on a random door and you all run away.

What time is it Mr Wolf

One player is the wolf and the rest have to sneak up and tap them on the shoulder. Different variations of this game include having to remain still and counting steps (the number of steps are the same number of the time the wolf says it is).

Manhunt.

Similar to Stokie.

Kiss chase.

Another self-explanatory game where someone chases you and if you get caught you receive a kiss.

Doctors and nurses.

I'm not sure of the rules of this game as I was always the ambulance driver.

Rhymes

To select teams to play the games listed, everyone gathered in a circle first of all. We all put a foot in and one person recited a rhyme and each word got you a tap on the foot until you were 'out' (or 'on'). If not tapped on the foot, it could be just a point of a finger per word.

Hip dip cow s***t, hip dip out

There's a party on the hill
Will you come?
Bring your own bread and butter
And a bun
Who is your best friend?

(Friends name is added to next part of rhyme)

—— will be there
with a ribbon in their hair
What colour will it be

(The letters of the colour are spelt out)

And you are not it

Ickle ockle chocolate bockle ickle ockle out.

Eeny, meeny, miny moe,
Catch a tiger by the toe.
If he squeals, let him go,
Eeny, meeny, miny moe.
Pig snout you are out.

One Patato, two potato, three potato, four
Five potato, six potato, seven potato, more.

Stokie name changes

Stokies are great at changing people's Christian names, Here are a few examples.

George – Gudda

Norman – Nunca

Harold – Adger

Brian – Brinter

Alan – Alg

Harry – H

Paul – Po

Albert / Norbert – Nobby

Derek – Decker

Eric – Ecker

Mickle – Michael

Maurice – Modger

Nigel – Nidge

Christian Patterson

The Stoke panto entertains thousands every year at The Regent Theatre up Hanley.

Each Christmas, Jonny Wilkes teams up with honorary Stokie Christian Patterson to put on one hell of a show.

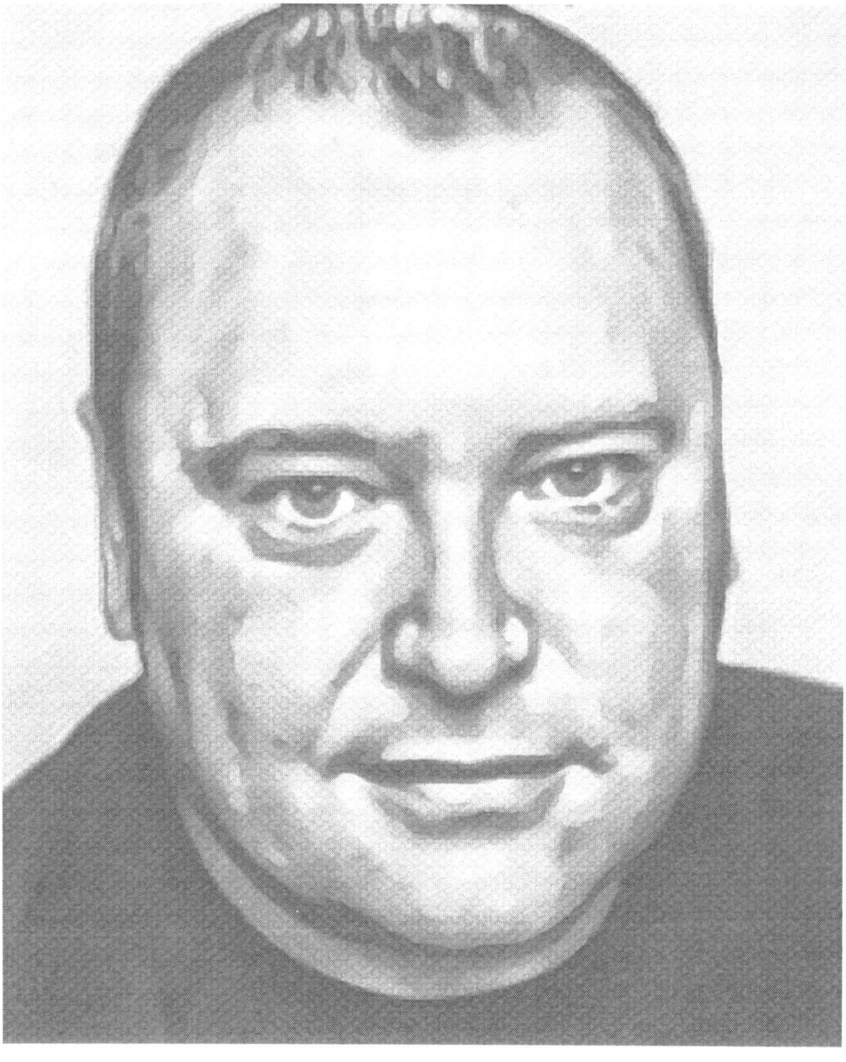

Christian spends a lot of time in the Potteries and told me a couple of his favourite stories from his times in the City Centre.

So...I was walking through Hanley on my way to work and I decided to get an oatcake from Kev's Van outside Boots (Oatie Moston's). There was a little queue and I was behind two old Stokie ladies. I wasn't eavesdropping but they were talking so loudly that you'd have been hard pressed not to hear what they were talking about. One of the ladies was telling the other that her friend Margaret had disturbed burglars in the house in the middle of the night. The other lady asked if there was much damage to which the first lady replied "No, not really, but they smashed her back doors in."
I nearly wet myself laughing and had to pretend I was having a severe coughing fit. When I got to the theatre I put a call out for all cast and crew to go to the main auditorium ASAP so I could tell them the story! Bloody brilliant!

Another one...

My wife wanted to buy her mother a gold cross on a chain for Christmas so I went up to H Samuels in Hanley. It was packed but eventually I got to the front of the queue. I told the young lady behind the counter that I was looking for a gold cross and she said "I've got quite a few I can show you...did you want a plain cross or one with the little man on?"

Crisp Addict by Nick Degg

Crisp Addict

Monster Munch and kettle chips
And savoury tomato Space ships
Skips, and Snaps and Bacon fries
Frazzles that dazzle and water the eyes
Chipsticks, Wotsits, Cheesey Puffs
Potato, Corn- Maize, and other stuffs
Taste sensations on your tongue
It feels so right, but it's all so wrong

Crispy crisp and crunchy crunch
Just one bag with your lunch
Squeeze the bags in the shop
To find the one thats full T't top

A BBQ Beef Hula Hoop
Makes an ideal crouton in Oxtail Soup
I need some crisps, I need them now
Flavoured pig, or cheese, or cow
Open the bag breathe it in
Or pop the top on a Pringles tin
Savour the flavour, Do us a favour
Lend s a quid I need a Quaver
Oooohhhh Crisps

I Love You

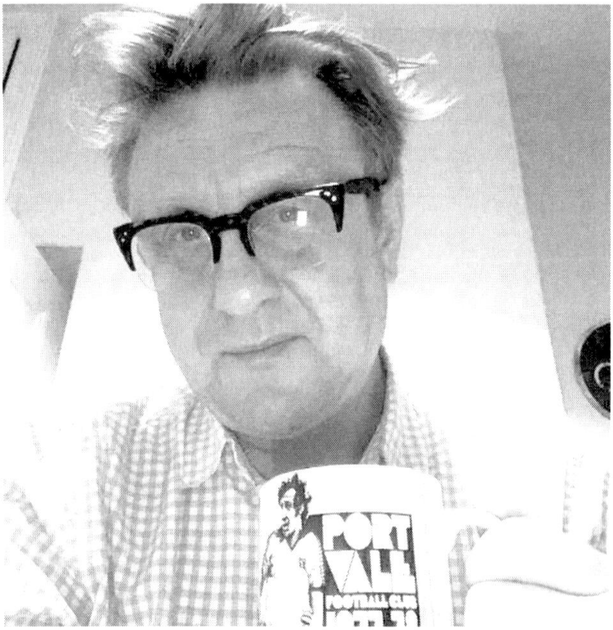

The Plank

Soooo, let's play a little game, what is this pictured and don't say planks of wood!

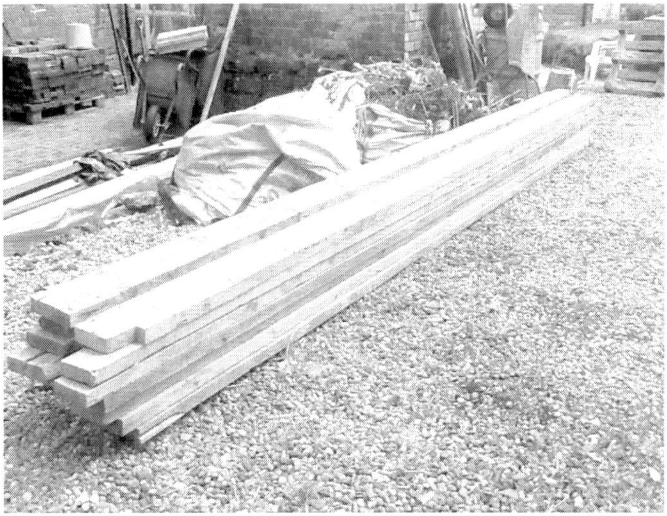

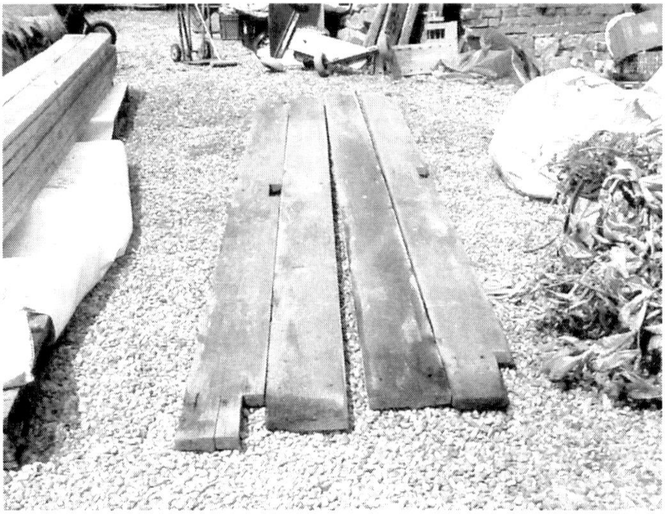

Answer at the back of the book...

The Beano

Stories from Dick Dale from the Port Vale fanzine The Beano:

John Jeffers

Over the last 23 years it's been a pleasure interviewing many ex Vale players for the Vale Park Beano. Some of their stories have been nothing less than hilarious and all of them have been extremely popular with our readers. It's hard to choose, but there's one player in particular I'll never forget.

John Jeffers had been a fans' favourite whilst at the Vale but since quitting football he'd started a new career in finance. He had a successful and profitable business in Liverpool where his staff were unaware of his past career when he played in front of thousands of spectators all over England. In building the business up. he'd put his playing days at Anfield and Vale Park behind him and never thought to bring up the subject with his employees. He'd moved on, and started afresh.

However, when I interviewed him he proved to be one of the most prolific interviewees I'd ever spoken to. I asked one question and that was it, he went from one subject to another hardly stopping to breathe. He was brilliant to listen to and he just loved reminiscing about his days as a footballer. Along with Russell Bromage, another outstanding ex-Vale favourite who could talk the hind leg off a donkey, the interview had to be split into three parts and were featured in three editions of the fanzine, numbers 70,71, and 72 back in 2010.

One of his tales concerned our neighbours down the D-Road. It was his first experience of playing in a Potteries derby and before the game Rudgie (manager John Rudge) took him aside telling him to be careful as the two clubs didn't play each other very often and he warmed him that when a game did take place it was an experience you'd remember for a long, long time.

The day of the match arrived and just a couple of minutes into the game, JJ was taking a throw-in when loads of agitated Stoke fans came running down shouting and swearing their heads off at him. He was more than shocked at the language and the behaviour as he'd never experienced anything like it before it, not even at a Liverpool v Everton game.

He went on to feature in a few derby games, the FA Cup replay in 1992 being of his favourites, and one of mine also of course.

Played in torrential rain he thought that he heard the half time whistle blow and quickly left the pitch to get a cup of warming tea. A ball boy ran up to him shouting, but Jinkin' Jeffers just thought the lad wanted to tell him he'd played well. Upon entering the dressing room Stan the kit man was astonished to see him and screamed at him to get back on the pitch as the game was still in progress. Amazed, he rejoined the game hoping that no one had noticed, however an eagle eyed Andy Grey who was commentating for TV had spotted the events and said he wondered where Jeffers had been.

That evening he went out on a bender with Swanny ending up in a pub somewhere in Newcastle. Singing 'one nil down– three one up, we knocked City out of the cup,'

They suddenly realised all the other drinkers had gone deathly quiet and for a good reason, they were all Stoke fans. Tables and pint pots were flying all over the place as they made a hasty exit. Needless to say they were far more careful where they drank after that.

When JJ first joined the Vale on loan in 1988 Mike Pejic took a training session. At the end of the session Pej asked Bob Hazell to collect the balls. In reply Big Bob told him in no uncertain terms that he could collect them himself. At that Pej then shouted at Bob to do 20 press up's. Again the answer was in the negative as Rudgie who was looking on, turned away shaking his head. Bob then said he was going back to Vale Park to warm up his piles on a radiator and walked off. For once Mike Pejic was speechless but JJ and Big Bob soon became firm friends until Bob left Port Vale.

John Jeffers was a good servant to the club. Some say he was a show off and over rated, others say he could have gone a lot further in football but whatever your opinion of him, he was a member of the club during its most successful period in recent history and there's no doubting that he played an important part in that success.

Robbie Earle

Everybody loved Robbie Earle and we all wished him well when he moved to Wimbledon for nearly a million pounds. He was a good honest player, but unfortunately for him his honesty cost him £5,000.

The season before he left Vale he went with the rest of the squad to Stirling University for pre-season training. The University was in the middle of nowhere, and the nearest pub was a taxi ride away.

Although Rudgie had told the lads they weren't allowed to go out for a drink, most of them including Robbie, booked a couple of taxi's and headed for the nearest boozer.

In the early hours they returned to the university the worst for wear, making such a racket that they woke up John Rudge. He was fuming and told them in no uncertain terms that he'd have strong words with them the following morning.

True to his word the next morning he informed them that he was sending them home in disgrace and they'd have to make their own way back. Somehow, probably due to a worker at the university, the press got to hear of it. There then followed media headlines saying 'Drunken Port Vale players sent home in shame,' together with articles greatly exaggerating what had actually happened.

In wasn't too long after this that Wimbledon came in for Robbie and he travelled to London to meet the club's owner Sam Hammam. The two clubs had already agreed a fee, all that was left to discuss was the signing on fee. At the meeting Sam brought up the subject of the events at Stirling University and asked Robbie if he had been involved in the drunken night out. Naturally Robbie denied any involvement pleading ignorance of the booze up and insisting he was in bed asleep when the others went out.

'That's a shame,' replied Sam Hammam, 'if you had been in the pub with the rest of them I'd have given you another five thousand quid on your signing on fee, as that is the sort of player I like at Wimbledon.'

Oatcake day

Stoke's a loada rubbish
What's left to do rind here?
The locals love to mumble
Into their Titanic beer

We've lost too many potbanks
There's no Disney store
My favourite pub is shutting
It's were loads better before

Ask yourself the question
What does keep you here?
The footys up and down
But the houses onner dear

We've had the best darts chuckers
The king of winning the Brits
Eddie was Worlds strongest mon
Even Slash loves us to bits

From Northern soul to raving
The wizard of the dribble
But the thing that unites us
Is a delicacy we like to nibble

Every August on the 8th
We remember pits and clay
So stand up for Stoke-on-Trent
And celebrate Oatcake Day

Lee Finan

ID104 was one of the most listened to nighttime radio shows outside of London in the mid to late 1990s. Hosted by 'Leaping' Lee Finan who came through the ranks at Signal Radio presenting shows across their schedule.

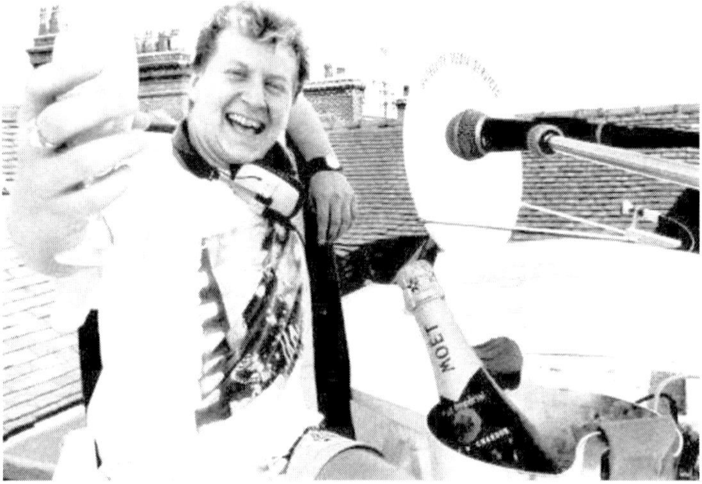

He released two solo records - 'You move too slow' and 'Nigel the gnome' and DJed at local nightclubs too. His tea boy at one point was none other than Robbie Williams who went on to do ok for himself too.

But as well as all this, he is remembered for getting the sack after not only reciting this rhyme, getting listeners to try it but also getting the travel person on air to have a go. The tongue twister in question trips most people up into a whole load of profanity. Lee went on to present across the country and still works in radio. When I asked for his permission to write about this, he gave his blessing saying what fond memories he has of the area. Have a go at the tongue twister yourself:

I'm not the pheasant plucker,
I'm the pheasant plucker's mate
And I'm only plucking pheasants
Cos the pheasant plucker's late.

Now say it faster!!!

High Lane

Pete Conway: A couple of years ago, Robbie's management rang me saying Ayda loves Pikelets so could I speak to Eileen to sort some?

I asked who Eileen was.

They said Eileen's oatcakes.

I said do you mean High Lane oatcakes?

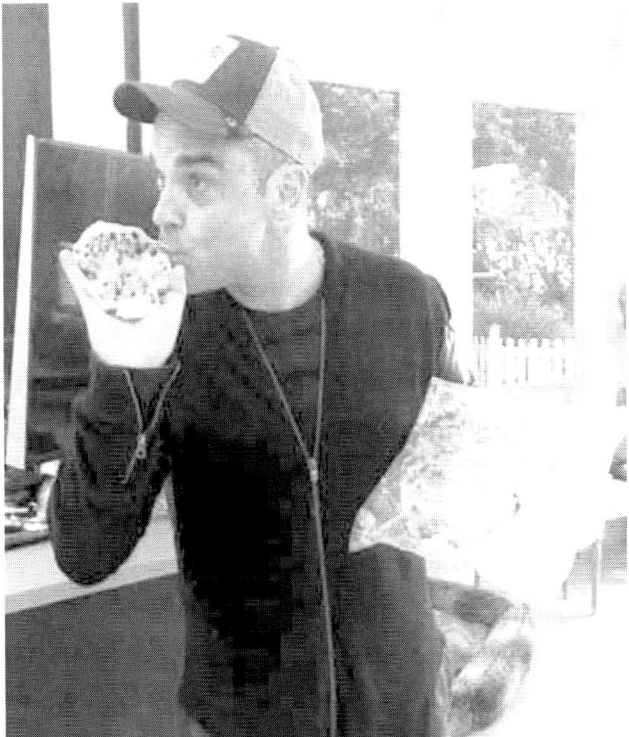

Stokeywood

Over the years, many TV and film production companies have looked at Staffordshire as a location for their project. Middleport Pottery recently housed the Peaky Blinders for their canal scenes in 2019. Gun shots were heard across the area and fans came from all over to try and get a glimpse of the stars. As well as the small screen, Hollywood has coming knocking on our doors.

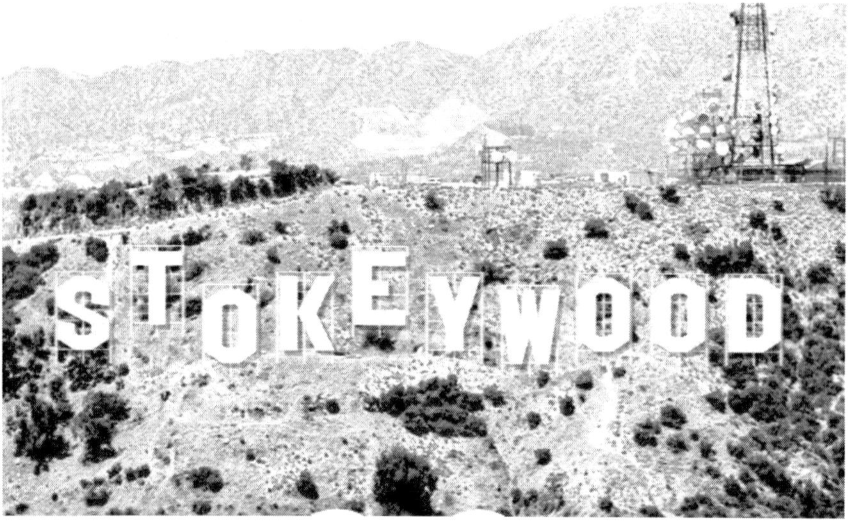

Here are six movies with scenes filmed in our area.

The Card - shot mainly in Burslem (aka Bursley) and starring Obi Wan Kenobi himself, Sir Alec Guinness.

Marvellous - the story of local hero, Neil 'Nello' Baldwin starring the awesome Toby Jones. Including scenes shot at Keele (although they used Crewe Alexandra's stadium to play The Victoria Ground).

Toby Jones (as himself) and Neil Baldwin as 'Nello':

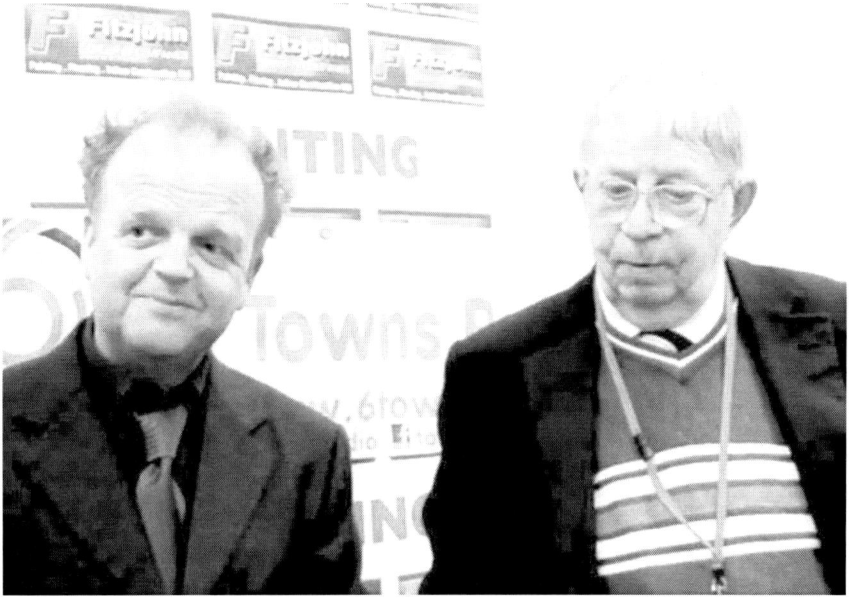

The Girl With All The Gifts - watch 'closely' as A-list actress Glenn Close walks past a sign for oatcakes inside the derelict old Hanley bus station.

The Smallest Show On Earth - shots of Longton can be seen through the train windows towards the end of this film that stars Peter Sellers.

Soulboy - The Kings Hall stars in this film playing Wigan Casino. Co-stars include Oscar nominated Felicity Jones and Huey from The Fun Lovin' Criminals.

The Silent Child - this Oscar winning film starring Rachel Shenton came out on Oatcake Day 2017. The movie has a backdrop of Caverswall, Longton Park and a place called 'rural England'.

Rumour mill: On IMDB, it says the ***Porridge*** movie starring Ronnie Barker has scenes shot at Stoke railway station. This wasn't released on Oatcake Day though, probably as the day didn't exist then. I can't spot Stoke in the film myself but if you know anything please email me: terrybossons@hotmail.com

The Thing!

Back in the early 80s, just down the road from where I lived, there was some graffiti that always intrigued me. Daubed on a cream window ledge at the bottom of Lawton Street in Biddulph were the words The Thing '83' in marker pen. For many years later I saw this tag all over the Potteries and some folk told me it dates back to the late 70s.

So who is 'The Thing?'. Was he the Stoke Banksy ahead of his time? A friend of mine went on a school trip in the 80s down Blue John Mines and 'The Thing' had etched his mark down there even.

Fast forward to 2020 and I had forgotten about this legend until my son asked me who 'The Thing' was? His friends were told an old wives tale about him being a scary character who roamed the streets at night. I wondered why he had asked and he told me he had seen graffiti, mainly on Virgin Media green boxes. So I ventured out that day and lo and behold I spotted 6 'The Thing 2020' tags whilst on a long walk. So is he back and more importantly who is he???

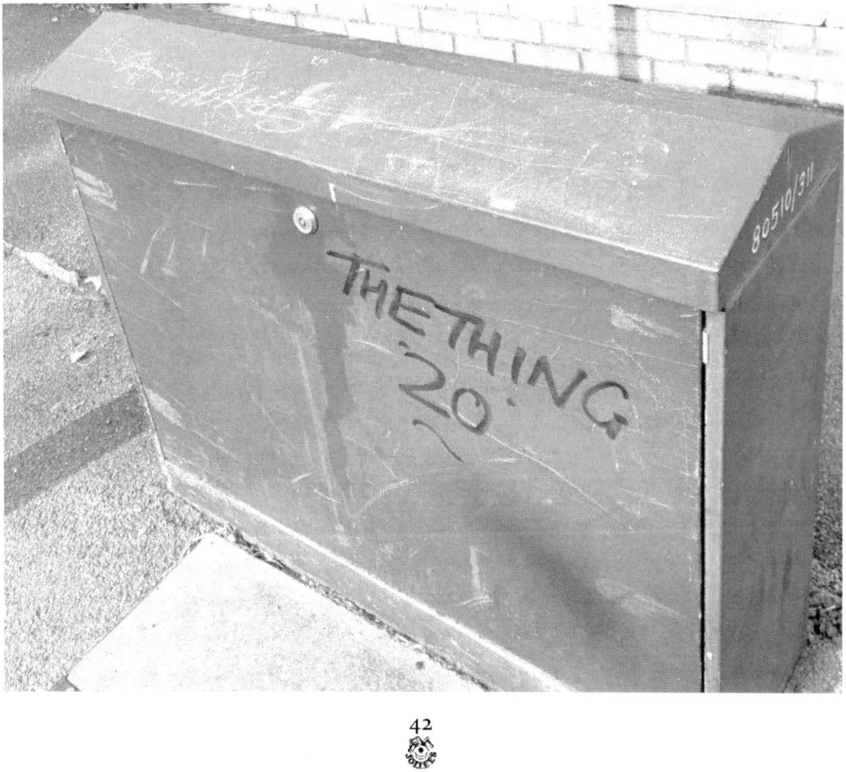

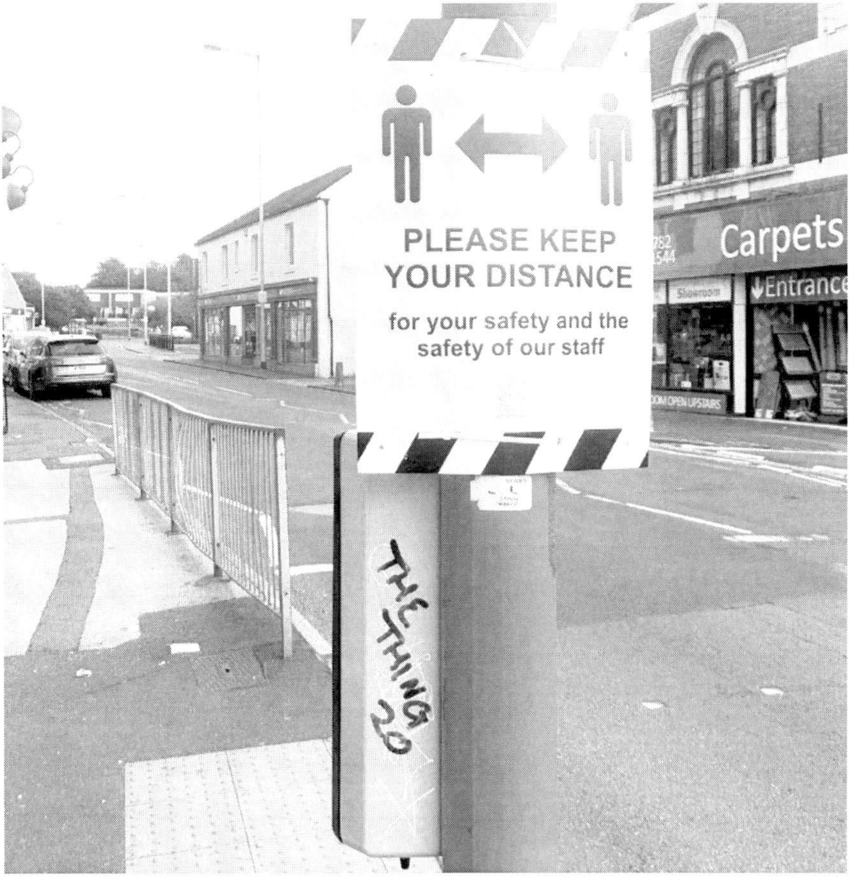
PLEASE KEEP
YOUR DISTANCE
for your safety and the
safety of our staff
Carpets
Entrance
Showroom
THE THING 20

Jackie Trent

Did you know that the hit TV soap, Neighbours nearly had a different name? But thanks to a local born singer, the title was changed just before it went on air.

Jackie Trent was born in Newcastle-under-Lyme in 1940, she sadly left us in 2015 but visited me a couple of years before to have a chat.

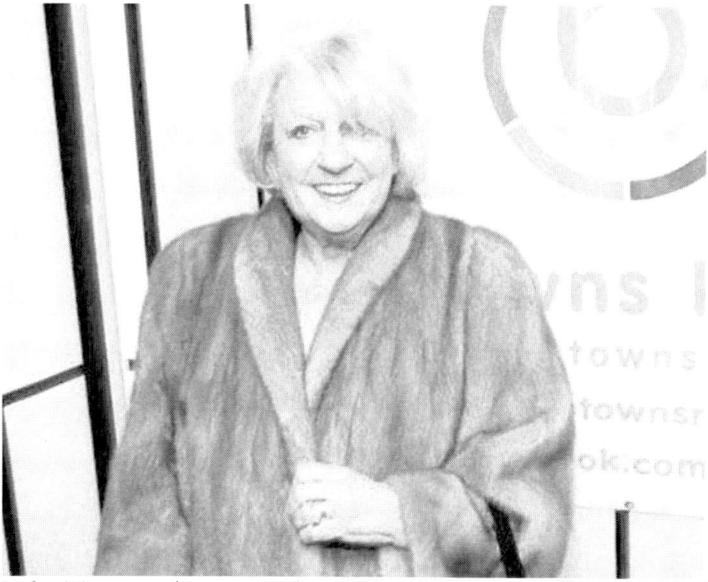

Whist Jackie Trent was living in Sydney with former husband Tony Hatch, they were approached by Grundy TV to write the theme for a new show. It was called 'Ramsey Street' and a storyboard was sent over with what the soap was about. Jackie thought that the show name was a bit close to Coronation Street, as it was set in a cul-de-sac it should focus on them being Neighbours she said. So her and Tony ran with the working title 'Neighbours, everybody needs good neighbours'.

She told me that they started on the song around 4pm, Tony upstairs in the studio laying the track down whilst Jackie prepped the dinner in the kitchen. She had a writing pad at hand and jotted down the lyrics. It was written and recorded by 11pm that night. They had called singer Barry Crocker over and he arrived in his dressing gown as he usually went to bed at 9pm.

It was with the Grundy TV company the next morning and they agreed that it should be called Neighbours. The rest, they say is history.

Satisfaction

In the mid 60s, all the big names of the time played in Stoke-on-Trent. Back then, Peter Williams was a police officer working in Hanley. This is long before he became the entertainer Pete Conway that we know and love.

He told me that one night they had the Rolling Stones at Hanley police station. They hadn't done anything wrong but would need to be sneaked into the Gaumont Theatre as the crowds in town were too much. So Pete and his fellow officers got the band into a police van and headed to the venue. They decided to get the van as close to the stage door as they could so they could slide the door open and get them in unscathed.

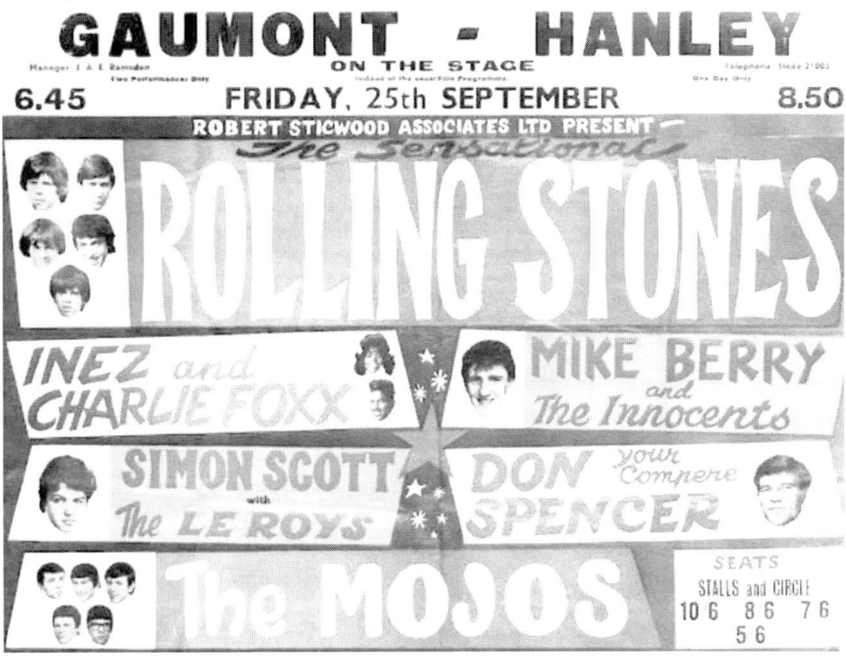

After the show, Mick Jagger and the boys asked the police where they could get a drink and Pete suggested The Place nightclub as he knew the head bouncer. So off they went only to be turned away by Pete's mate for wearing jeans.

[The above poster sold recently at Bonhams for £10,200!]

Stoke Con Trent

Stoke Con Trent is a film, TV and media convention that has taken place at Staffordshire University since 2014. TV guests have included the cast of Red Dwarf, Allo Allo, Gavin & Stacey, Game of Thrones Doctor Who, Bottom, Gladiators and Only Fools And Horses.

John Challis who played Boycie in Only Fools And Horses has attended a few times and was at the very first event. He is a very popular guest as he has also appeared in Doctor Who and Benidorm too so is highly in demand for his autograph.

He recounts the first Stoke Con Trent to me as it was opened by his hero, former England goalkeeper Gordon Banks. The pair had a good chat and posed for a photo (below).

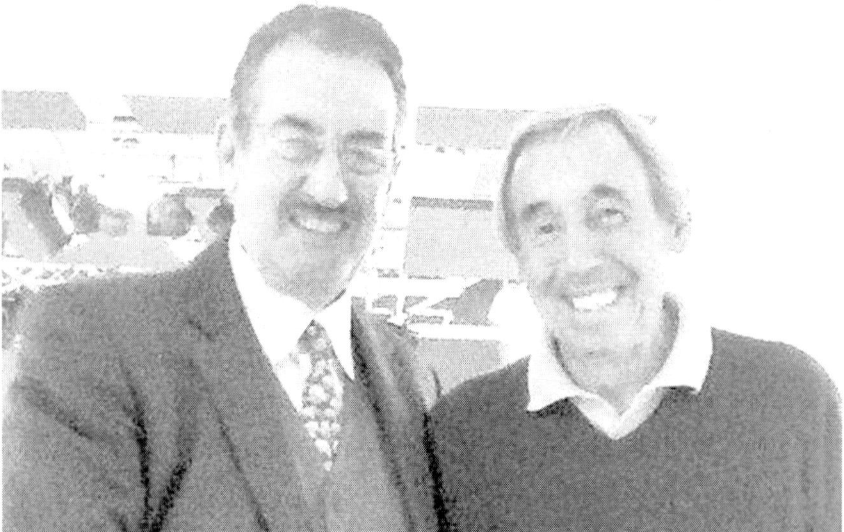

John told me:
Obviously I said that the World Cup win was the most wonderful day and he answered "We had a bit of luck and played OK."

I'm sure Gordon was equally in awe of meeting the sitcom legend.

Quiz

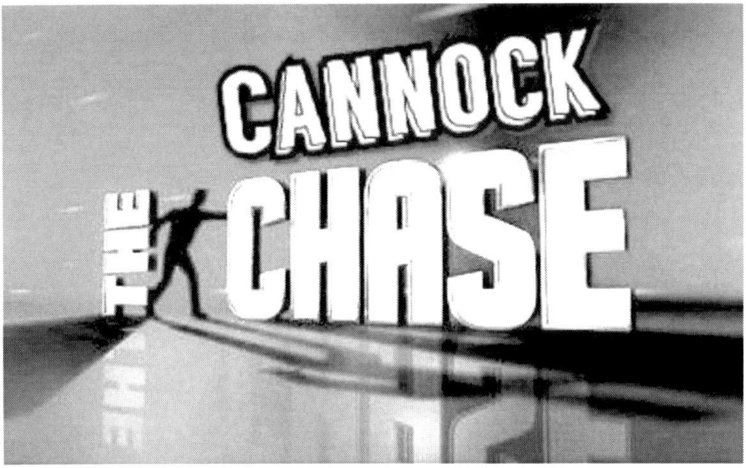

1. What connects Pete Conway to the late comedian Jim Bowen?
2. Which comedian was on Port Vale's books in the 1960s as a goalkeeper?
3. How did Lemmy get his famous nickname?
4. What popular ITV show did Jonathan Wilkes present from 2003 to 2004?
5. How did Slash get his famous nickname?
6. What does radio host Bruno Brookes have tattooed on his left thigh?
7. Which famous Potteries footballers' father was a professional boxer known as 'The Fighting Barber'?
8. Newcastle-under-Lyme born, Yvonne Ann Burgess had a brief fling with Elvis Presley. By what name was she better known?
9. What was darts legend Phil Taylor's nickname before he became 'The Power'?
10. Why is the A500 known as 'The D road'?

(see back of book for answers!)

As a...

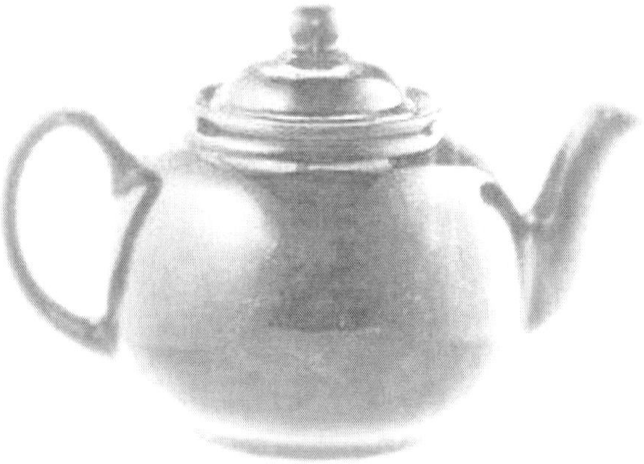

You've all been there as a kid, sitting there minding your own business. Then mum or dad comes in complaining about the mess in your room or the lack of chores you have done.

You hear the famous line:
"You're as much use as ..."

A chocolate fireguard.
A wet weekend in Wales.
An ashtray on a motorcycle.
A one legged man in an ass kicking contest.
A chocolate teapot.
A newspaper raincoat.
A waterproof teabag.
A lead parachute.
An inflatable dartboard.
Non-stick cellotape.
A glass hammer.
Roll on hairspray.
An ejector seat in a helicopter.

Which one were you?

The Record Collector.

The Record Collector by Ian Ledgar

You'll see him at car boot sales,
In charity shops and jumble sales,
Any chance to buy,
He's there, never fail,

He's hunting for his prey,
Knows what he's searching for,
If he could, he'd do it everyday,
Scrambling on the floor.

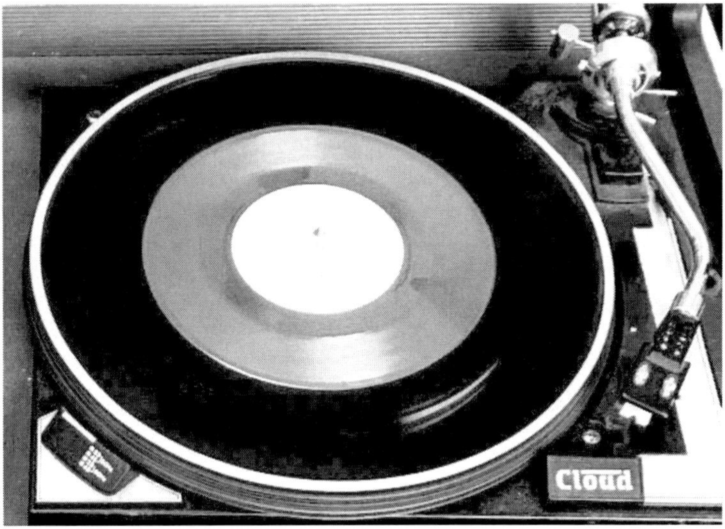

When he's on a dig,
There's no stopping him,
If he finds any he's after,
His demeanor changes,
A smile, close to laughter.

Every town he visits,
He's digging again,
The Record Collector,
How do I know?
It's me, I'm that man!

When I Grow Up

Since the age of nine, I've always wanted to be a DJ. Every penny I had was spent on records and I listened to the radio for hours and looked out for every music programme on TV. It became on obsession which it still is.

Obviously, I wanted to be a footballer like most kids in the 80s but the challenge of not being good enough got in the way.

This might sound unbelievable but I was a really shy kid, this was gonna be my only hurdle as DJs were seen as confident and chatty. So in 1987 I was given my first break at the local youth centre in Biddulph. The youth leaders - Barbara, Gloria, Brian and Wendy must have been desperate or I must have been persistent but I got a gig. They had their own equipment so I just needed to turn up with some records. There were a few people on the dancefloor I recall so I thought I would hit them with 'Never gonna give you up' whilst summoning the courage to use the microphone for the first time. The song was ending so I grabbed the mic and said "That was Rick Astley!". Before I had chance to continue my patter a girl stood three feet away said "You don't say!". Well the song was at number one, but that first heckle didn't hold me back.

Going back to being shy, I was usually a bag of nerves going on stage. A prep talk to the mirror in the toilets usually took place after the odd nervous vomit.

After a couple of years DJing at the youth centre, Town Hall and on the SPACE scheme I wanted to get a pub gig. In 1989, aged seventeen I asked DJ Trevor Lancaster if I could spin a few songs at his gig at The Roebuck in Biddulph. He agreed as this gave him chance to chat to all the ladies gathered around the DJ booth. Not long after, DJ Adam Gold let me loose at The Top of the Trent and even let me fill in for him when he couldn't do it. This was my baptism of fire, the pub had a reputation for being rough so I had to up my game and somehow infiltrated in with the locals.

In 1990, I got my first night club gig - The Valiant club in Burslem. This came around about the same time as I became good friends with a DJ called Coco who did The Crafty Cockney. The Cockney was such a fun place and I wanted to bring this atmosphere to Hamil Road. Again this place didn't suffer fools and it certainly opened my eyes to what a pub brawl looked like. The manager, Mike Gittins took to me and when he opened a bar he called me in to work in the Mecca of Potteries nightlife - Hanley!

The Manhattan bar became a thing of legend amongst the party people of Stoke-on-Trent. It was only small, but with it's Sky football, party music and the 50p shots it was rammed four nights a week. As a kid, working in Hanley was my goal, I used to go to the top teens night on Sundays and watch in awe as DJ Trevor M entertained the masses at The Place. The Manhattan was ten years of gold - hardly any trouble and at the time when The Place and Valentino's were always chocka, it was a magical era. There are lots of stories to tell from this time, but I think it's for another book haha. My career led to gigs at Rosie O'Briens and Fluid along the way. I have always been very grateful for the opportunities I have been given.

Flares bar Hanley opened in 2002 and I was asked to cover a Sunday night on my 30th birthday and remember thinking it wouldn't be for me. How wrong could I be? Flares was so much fun and it was the perfect 'guilty pleasure' bar for those who didn't take life too seriously.

Yates's bar was next door and it wasn't long before I got a gig there. The boss at the time was called Kirk and he always used to tell me that DJing was 'money for old rope'. I told him that I made it look easy, which I always have. My constant challenge to get him to give it a go never materialised strangely.

So fast forward to 2020 and I'm still working in Hanley at Reflex as well as Yates in Newcastle under Lyme and Stafford. I don't want to massage their egos too much but my managers - Stuart, Robin and Ash are all a joy to work for. This goes for all the bosses I've had really, it's team work at the end of the day.

People say to me that going out isn't what it used to be, but they've said this to me for thirty years!

Pottersaurus update

Aart - out
Abite - about
Adoo? - how do you do?
Afoor - before
Arint - around
Arlav- I will have
Arnoo - I know
Assayneet? - have you seen it?
Asstrardeet? - have you tried it?
Ast? - have you?
Aych - each
Ayes - eyes
Aynuff - enough
Barmy on the crumpet - not all there
Baysides - besides
Bed clothes - bed sheets
Beaked up - dirty
Beowred - bored
Betwayne - between
Bin yer? - how have you been?
Blab - gossip
Bode - bald
Bool- bowl
Borred- borrowed
Borreler pop - a bottle of pop
Bosco - mouth
Bowd - bowled
Brass knocker onner pig-sty door - A gold ring on a dirty hand
Brine - brown
Bull wik - the week you tried to get more pay to boost holiday pay
Bureetinnerupternay - but it isn't up to me
Caylin - ceiling
Chimlee- chimney
Clayn - clean
Cleow - clue
Cleowsin - closing
Coat up - caught up

Cock wood - it's guaranteed that if you take these bits of wood home you will get some action
Comical dick - someone who changes their mind
Connabearim - I can't stand him
Coss - curse
Craysed - creased
Crog- clumsy kick
Cupatay - cup of tea
Cuther - gossip
Daft Apeth - a daft person
Deowin - doing
Dinger - naughty boy
Divil - devil
Dooers- doors
Draym- dream
Dust - do
Farndin - finding
Fassen- fasten
Favereet - favourite
Fayer- fire
Fayt - feet
Fayver - fiver
Feece - face
Feowse - fuse
Flittin - to move house
Flooer - floor
Foe bits - fall to bits
Fogsy - nominate yourself to go first
Fond - found
Foteneet - fortnight
Fowad- forward
Franked - late for work
Frittened deeth - someone who was really frightened
Furrum- for them
Ghosbosterz - Ghostbusters
Goreet - got it
Gotter- got to
Grind - ground
Ight- out
Jed - dead
Kaggy - left handed

Ketch - catch
Late - light
Layve- leave
Leedy - lady
Lils - boobs
Little nowt - naughty kid
Maul - move something heavy
Made away - dirty
May ode blister- my old pal
Mayl - mile
Maynst - mean
Mayzin - amazing
Member - remember
Menny - many
Mind - don't forget
Moggy - cat
Mon - man
Monstink - a show off
Narnin cheese - nine inches
Necks - next
Nedna- need not
Neow- new
Nother - another
N'nall - as well
Oh Onyer - all of you
Onds - hands
One off eight? - want a fight?
Onner bayin wotsit larke - I aren't being funny
Orts - left overs
Osses- horses
Owat? - how are you?
Owd hat - just old
Oweeys - always
Owter - how to
Poses - posts
Payce - piece
Pays - peas
Peedee - pay day
Pee - pay
Photer- photo
Pickcher - picture

Piece (payce)- sarnie
Pitcher arsed - feeling fragile
Pittle - wee
Playze - please
Pleet- plate
Pon - pan
Pooley bad - ill
Pureet- put it
Quate- quiet
Raydin- reading
Reens - rains
Remind me on - remind me
Reowm- room
Rexfur- ask for
Saffog - a smelly
Seele - sale
Seer - it's here
Segsy - to nominate oneself to go second
Sester- sister
Sheows - shoes
Showned - to show around
Shotties - marbles
Skinches - crossed fingers
Slobber chops - messy eater
Sneak - snake
Sometarms - sometimes
Sowgers - soldiers
Spom - spam
Spon new - brand new
Spout - it's about
Steek - steak
Stheer - it's there
Stond - stand
Stuneen - stunning
Sut - sat
Sarnd - sound
Tackit dine - take it down
Tallin - telling
Taters - potatos
Tay - tea
Teeble - table

Ter - to
Terdee - today
Tharriz - that is
Thayter - Theatre
Thes - this
They astner ast? - you haven't, have you?
Theyat - you are
Thut - that
Tinner- it isn't
Tinker - naughty kid
Tittle - tickle
Trard - tried
Trashers - shoes
Tray - tree
Umpteenth - a lot of times
Wakes wik - wakes week
Wayne - wine
Whale - while
Wikend- weekend
Wiks - weeks
Winder - window
Wirk- work
Wo peeper - wall paper
Wanna do owt? - do you want to do something?
Wonteet? - wasn't it?
Worrabite? - what about?
Wazya? - were you?
Wudna? - wouldn't
Wrostle - wrestle
Wull - well
Wunce- once
Wut? - would you?

Answer to The Plank?
It's the original stage from Jollees! Still to this day stored in someone's back garden.

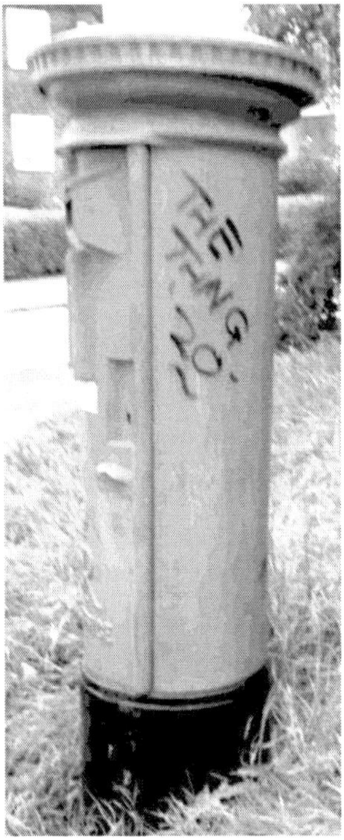

Quiz Answers:
1. They were both christened Peter Williams
2. Mick Miller.
3. He loved slot machines and said to friends 'lemmy a fiver until Friday'.
4. You've been framed.
5. Actor Seymour Cassel gave him the nickname because he thought Slash was perpetually working on his next hustle or scheme.
6. A pirate.
7. Sir Stanley Matthews.
8. Jackie Trent.
9. The Crafty Potter.
10. D is the Roman numeral for 500. The road does make the vague shape of a D with theM6 motorway, but that's not the reason for its name.

Thank you's

My mum, Gran, Amy Bossons, Connor Bossons, Jaxxon Bossons, Arnie, Shelby, Bec, Sam, Effy, Boss, Nana & Grandad Shaw, John Thompson, Jan Thompson, Dave Lee, Dylan Lee, Ezra, Kirst, Biff, Rich 'The Man' Hughes, Dan Townley, Joe Edwards, Ross Irving, Paul Rutter, Rich Hughes, Fred Hughes, Pete Conway, Adrian Tooth, John Acres, Matt Lee, Louise Stones, Jason Dale, The Talbies, Den Siegurtsz, Ian Hudson, Merrym'n, The Trent Vale Poet, Christian Patterson, Martin Tideswell, Cannon and Ball, Rob Ledgar, Chris Burton, Jimmy Cricket, Dick Dale, The Theatre Royal Facebook group, Dave Johnson, Simon Lindop, Alan May, Craig Longson, Stan Boardman, Lee Finan, Ian Ledgar, Darren Anstey, Neil Hood, Phil McGraw, The Grumbleweeds, Jollees, Mel Scholes, Bethan Rose, Gail Peters, Gary Ellerton, Owd Grandad Piggott, May Un mar lady, Alan Povey, Nick Degg, Slash, Robbie, Phil Taylor, Jackie Trent, 'The Thing', Hanley Museum, Boycie, Music Mania and The World Wide Web.

In memory of Shaun Kelly, Dean Tyson and Shaun Nicholls ❤

"The only GCSE's I have are on my CV"

Terry Bossons August 2020

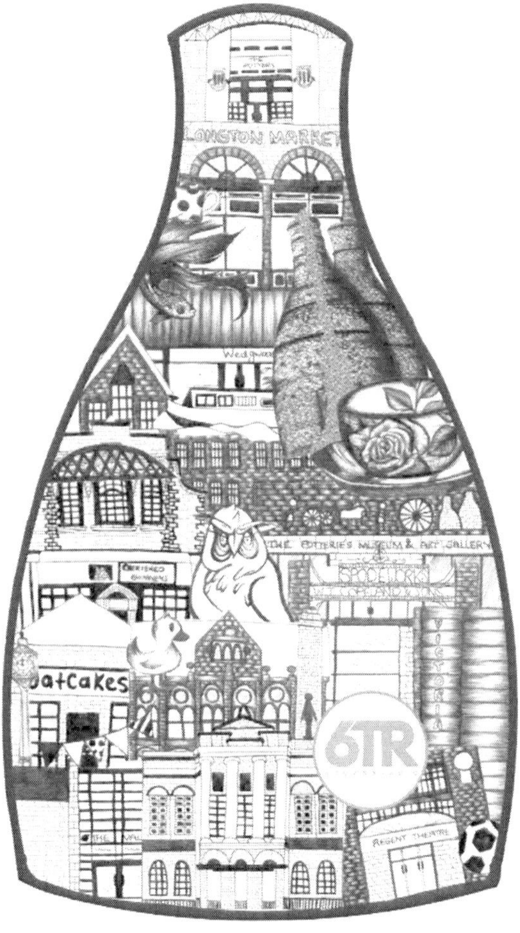

Megan Rose Design

Happy Birthday 6 Towns Radio 2010 – 2020

For more images like this and to buy prints visit: https://meganrosedesign.co.uk/

INDEX